IT'S ELEMEN

For a character first introduced in print in 1887, Sherlock Holmes is still going strong. Generations of readers and mystery aficionados have enjoyed the adventures of the sleuth and his sidekick, Dr. Watson, as well as numerous stage and screen adaptations. Those adventures were the inspiration for this book, *Sherlock Holmes Puzzles.*

Do you have Sherlock Holmes' keen eyes and attention to detail? You can prove it by solving mystery-themed visual puzzles. Do you have his logical abilities? The book offers logic puzzles, cryptograms, and more. Along the way, you'll also get to test your knowledge of the Doyle canon with plenty of Holmes trivia.

Don't worry if you find yourself getting stuck occasionally—even Watson needed a bit of explanation from time to time! Answers are located at the back of the book when you need a helpful boost. So grab your pencil—and a deerstalker cap, if you'd like—and get ready to detect.

A "SOL OHM HECKLERS" ANAGRAM

Below is a quotation from a Sherlock Holmes story. Fill in the blanks in each sentence with a word that is an anagram (rearrangement) of the capitalized word(s).

BONUS: Name the Sherlock Holmes adventure from which this quotation is drawn.

"Really, Watson, you excel SOLE FURY _____," said Holmes, pushing back his chair and lighting a cigarette. "I am bound to say that in all the NO CACTUS _____ which you have been so good as to give of my own small CAVEMEN HEIST _____ you have habitually RUNE TRADED _____ your own abilities. It may be that you are not yourself US UM LION _____, but you are a conductor of light. Some people without SIS SPONGES _____ genius have a remarkable power of SAILING MUTT _____ it. I confess, my dear ELF OWL _____, that I am very much in your debt."

Answers on page 171.

A STUDY IN SHERLOCK

Complete each quote from "A Study in Scarlet" with one of the choices.

1. "How are you?" he said cordially, gripping my hand with a strength for which I should hardly have given him credit. "You have been in _____, I perceive."

    A. Afghanistan

    B. Devonshire

    C. hospital

2. His _____ was as remarkable as his knowledge.

    A. range of interests

    B. curiosity

    C. ignorance

3. There was one little sallow rat-faced, dark-eyed fellow who was introduced to me as _____, and who came three or four times in a single week.

    A. Inspector Gregson

    B. Mr. Lestrade

    C. Inspector Lestrade

4. "By a man's finger nails, by his coat-sleeve, by his boot, by his trouser knees, by the callosities of his forefinger and thumb, by his expression, by his shirt cuffs—by each of these things a man's _____ is plainly revealed."

    A. calling

    B. address

    C. location

5. "No doubt you think that you are complimenting me in comparing me to _____," he observed. "Now, in my opinion, _____ was a very inferior fellow.

    A. Lecoq

    B. Bertillon

    C. Dupin

Answers on page 171.

FOR STAGE AND SCREEN

Every name below belongs to an actor who played the role of Watson in a Sherlock Holmes adaptation. Names can be found in a straight line horizontally, vertically, or diagonally. They may be read either forward or backward.

ALAN COX

BEN KINGSLEY

BRUCE MCRAE

COLIN BLAKELY

DAVID BURKE

DONALD PICKERING

EDWARD HARDWICKE

H. KYRLE BELLEW

HUBERT WILLIS

JUDE LAW

MARTIN FREEMAN

NIGEL BRUCE

PATRICK MACNEE

RAYMOND FRANCIS

ROBERT DUVALL

ROLAND YOUNG

```
D O N A L D P I C K E R I N G
A K K B N B R U C E M C R A E
V R A Y M O N D F R A N C I S
I Q Y X O C N A L A Q Q Y R R
D G N U O Y D N A L O R W O F
B E N K I N G S L E Y H F B B
U I N I G E L B R U C E X E V
R T R H T F Q S C D Q J S R M
K W P O J X D Y R Y U V I T H
E K C I W D R A H D R A W D E
M A R T I N F R E E M A N U I
W E L L E B E L R Y K H C V T
H X E E N C A M K C I R T A P
S I L L I W T R E B U H M L V
W J M C O L I N B L A K E L Y
```

Answers on page 171.

FINGERPRINT MATCH

There are 4 sets of fingerprints. Find each match.

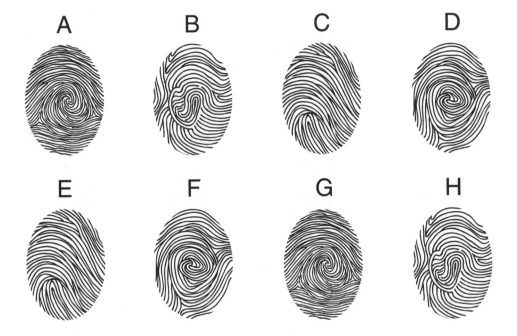

Answers on page 171.

WHAT WENT MISSING? (PART I)

The consulting detective met his client on Thursday, and was told that a family heirloom, a diamond, was hidden somewhere in the room because the client had received demands for it. This was the room in which they met. Examine the room, then turn the page.

WHAT WENT MISSING? (PART II)

The next day, the consulting detective was called back because his client had disappeared. The consulting detective noted that something else had gone missing. From memory, can you work out what went missing?

Answer on page 171.

FOR HIS GENERATION

Cryptograms are messages in substitution code. Break the code to read the message. For example, THE SMART CAT might become FVO QWGDF JGF if **F** is substituted for **T**, **V** for **H**, **O** for **E**, and so on.

VITIDN LTIRR AEMNIJ RXI SEIQRX WC M EBCY-TQC-CWCY RIEIPWSWBC SITWIS ATBJQKIJ LN YTMCMJM RIEIPWSWBC WC RXI IWYXRWIS MCJ CWCIRWIS. ZBTRN-RGB BZ MTRXQT KBCMC JBNEI'S SRBTWIS GITI MJMARIJ ZBT RXI SITWIS, MCJ RXI SITWIS XMJ M TIAQRMRWBC ZBT LIWCY ZMWRXZQE RB RXI LBBFS. LTIRR XMJ MKRQMEEN AEMNIJ GMRSBC WC 1980, MKTBSS ZTBD KXMTERBC XISRBC'S XBEDIS.

NOTHING TO DO WITH DOYLE

Cryptograms are messages in substitution code. Break the code to read the message. For example, THE SMART CAT might become FVO QWGDF JGF if **F** is substituted for **T**, **V** for **H**, **O** for **E**, and so on.

C.C. CLHIBR VGRK'S G JDYSDLKGH NBSBYSDUB— CB VGR G RBQDGH FDHHBQ, LJSBK YLKRDNBQBN SCB JDQRS DK GIBQDYG. PLQK CBQIGK VBPRSBQ ITNABSS DK 1861, CB YLKJBRRBN SL 27 ITQNBQR PTS IGX CGUB PBBK QBRMLKRDPHB JLQ ILQB. CB VGR GHRL G PDAGIDRS, IGQQDBN SL SCQBB VLIBK GS SCB SDIB LJ CDR NBGSC.

Answers on page 172.

ART THEFTS

The city of Arbourg is on high alert after a series of brazen art thefts. Four different artworks were stolen in the past several months, each by a different artist, and each housed in a different museum. Help the police track down clues by matching each stolen artwork to its artist and the museum in which it was housed, and determining the month in which each was stolen.

1. The painting by Laurent Lafayette was stolen sometime after *City Dreams.*

2. *Apple Cart* was stolen one month before the piece by Pedro Pocalini went missing.

3. The painting by Stephan Strauss went missing sometime before June.

4. The Tendrille museum was robbed in May, just one month after the painting by Don De Lorenzo was stolen.

5. The Givernelle museum was robbed 2 months before *Elba at Dawn* went missing.

6. The Beaufort museum was robbed sometime before July.

		Titles				Artists				Museums			
		Apple Cart	City Dreams	Elba at Dawn	Madame V.	De Lorenzo	Lafayette	Pocalini	Strauss	Beaufort	Givernelle	Millefoi	Tendrille
Months	April												
	May												
	June												
	July												
Museums	Beaufort												
	Givernelle												
	Millefoi												
	Tendrille												
Artists	De Lorenzo												
	Lafayette												
	Pocalini												
	Strauss												

Months	Titles	Artists	Museums
April			
May			
June			
July			

13

Answers on page 172.

INTERCEPTION

You've intercepted a message that is meant to reveal a location for an upcoming meeting between two criminal masterminds. The only problem is, the message shows many place names. Can you figure out the right location?

WASHINGTON D.C.

PHNOM PENH

HELSINKI

FOND DU LAC

ATLANTA

PHILIPSBURG

OSLO

Answer on page 172.

A "SHH CELLO SMOKER" ANAGRAM

Below is a quotation from a Sherlock Holmes story. Fill in the blanks in each sentence with a word that is an anagram (rearrangement) of the capitalized word(s).

BONUS: Name the Sherlock Holmes adventure from which this quotation is drawn.

"No, no. No crime," said Sherlock Holmes, laughing. "Only one of those SWAM CHILI _____ little INSECT DIN _____ which will happen when you have four million human beings all JOG LINTS _____ each other within the space of a few square miles. Amid the action and reaction of so dense a swarm of HAM UNITY _____, every possible INACTION MOB _____ of events may be expected to take place, and many a little problem will be presented which may be GRIN SKIT _____ and BRAZIER _____ without being criminal. We have DARE LAY _____ had experience of such."

Answers on page 172.

THE HOUND OF THE BASKERVILLES

Each word or phrase in all capitals in the Sherlock Holmes quotation below is contained within the group of letters. Words can be found horizontally, vertically, or diagonally. They may read either forward or backward.

"I find that before the TERRIBLE event occurred several people had seen a CREATURE upon the MOOR which corresponds with this BASKERVILLE demon, and which could not possibly be any ANIMAL known to SCIENCE. They all agreed that it was a huge creature, LUMINOUS, GHASTLY, and SPECTRAL. I have CROSS-EXAMINED these men, one of them a HARD-HEADED countryman, one a FARRIER, and one a moorland FARMER, who all tell the same story of this dreadful APPARITION, exactly corresponding to the HELL-HOUND of the LEGEND. I assure you that there is a REIGN OF TERROR in the district, and that it is a hardy man who will cross the moor at night."

```
P D A D Q O D C C O W C Q G P
X E P E C L R F V H G D H R O
J D P N J D U A K C G A E O Y
U A A I A W F L A U S I S G Y
T E R M N J A R B T G Q B L S
E H I A I D S Z L N Z A A U E
L D T X M N Y Y O X S R O C F
B R I E A E P F Q K T N N E A
I A O S L G T A E C I E V N R
R H N S N E E R E M I H S L R
R Y J O R L V P U C M S U X I
E E T R T I S L S M K E Q L E
T Q O C L H A H O F A R M E R
C R O L D N U O H L L E H U P
C R E A T U R E G I T G H X S
```

                    Answers on page 172.

CRACK THE PASSWORD

A detective has found a memory aid that the criminal left behind, a list of coded passwords. The detective knows that the criminal likes to scramble each password, then remove the same letter from each word. Can you figure out the missing letter and unscramble each word in this set to reveal the passwords?

SINE

PRIMERS

LEARN

MICAS

IN OTHER WORDS

Cryptograms are messages in substitution code. Break the code to read the message. For example, THE SMART CAT might become FVO QWGDF JGF if **F** is substituted for **T,** **V** for **H, O** for **E,** and so on.

KWDGDWCK RGJ CWKLZJVGOK VDPAOFZ KZPJZL, ZDVMCYLVP, ROJLVQZ, KTYFGSW, PJWHLVP, YDF PAYDFZKLVDZ.

          Answers on page 173.

WHAT WENT MISSING? (PART I)

The consulting detective met his client on Monday, and was told that some old family documents were hidden somewhere in the room. This was the room in which they met. Examine the room, then turn the page.

WHAT WENT MISSING? (PART II)

On Tuesday, the consulting detective was called back because his client had disappeared. The consulting detective noted that something else had gone missing. From memory, can you work out what went missing?

Answer on page 173.

FAMOUS FIRST LINES

How well do you know the Holmes canon? Match the first line of each story to the story's title.

1. Mr. Sherlock Holmes, who was usually very late in the mornings, save upon those not infrequent occasions when he was up all night, was seated at the breakfast table.

2. In the year 1878 I took my degree of Doctor of Medicine of the University of London, and proceeded to Netley to go through the course prescribed for surgeons in the army.

3. Sherlock Holmes took his bottle from the corner of the mantel-piece and his hypodermic syringe from its neat morocco case.

4. To Sherlock Holmes she is always THE woman.

5. I had called upon my friend, Mr. Sherlock Holmes, one day in the autumn of last year and found him in deep conversation with a very stout, florid-faced, elderly gentleman with fiery red hair.

A. The Sign of the Four

B. A Scandal in Bohemia

C. The Hound of the Baskervilles

D. A Study in Scarlet

E. The Red-Headed League

Answers on page 173.

THE MISSING MILLIONAIRE

A wealthy oil tycoon named Allen Avery has gone missing, and his family has put up a huge reward for his safe return. Four different witnesses claim to have seen a man matching Avery's description in the past week, each in a different city and state. Using only the clues below, help track down Mr. Avery's whereabouts by matching each witness's sighting to its city, state, and date.

1. The California sighting occurred sometime after Edna Eddel's.

2. Avery was seen in Oregon 2 days after someone saw him in the town of Tetley.

3. Avery was seen in Ballingford sometime before Susie Seuss's reported sighting (which wasn't on Wednesday).

4. The sighting in Nevada was either the one by Hilda Hayes or the one on Tuesday (but not both).

5. Allen Avery was seen in Ventura 2 days after Edna Eddel's sighting.

6. Of Friday's witness report and the one in Washington state, one was in the city of Ventura and the other was submitted by Walt Wolsen.

	Witnesses				Cities				States			
	Edna Eddel	Hilda Hayes	Susie Seuss	Walt Wolsen	Ballingford	Pescadero	Tetley	Ventura	California	Nevada	Oregon	Washington
Days Tuesday												
Wednesday												
Thursday												
Friday												
States California												
Nevada												
Oregon												
Washington												
Cities Ballingford												
Pescadero												
Tetley												
Ventura												

Days	Witnesses	Cities	States
Tuesday			
Wednesday			
Thursday			
Friday			

Answers on page 173.

A "SMELL OH SHOCKER" ANAGRAM

Below is a quotation from a Sherlock Holmes story. Fill in the blanks in each sentence with a word that is an anagram (rearrangement) of the capitalized word(s).

BONUS: Name the Sherlock Holmes adventure from which this quotation is drawn.

I had neither kith nor kin in England, and was therefore as free as Air—or as free as an COIN ME _____ of eleven shillings and sixpence a day will TRIP ME _____ a man to be. Under such circumstances, I naturally gravitated to London, that great COP SOLES _____ into which all the LOSER GNU _____ and idlers of the Empire are irresistibly drained. There I stayed for some time at a RAVE TIP _____ hotel in the Strand, leading a FORCES MOLTS _____, meaningless existence, and spending such money as I had, considerably more EEL FRY _____ than I ought. So MARGINAL _____ did the state of my SCAN FINE _____ become, that I soon realized that I must either leave the metropolis and CRATE SUIT _____ somewhere in the country, or that I must make a complete ALIEN TAROT _____ in my style of living. Choosing the latter alternative, I began by making up my mind to leave the hotel, and to take up my quarters in some less ENTRIES POUT _____ and less expensive ICED LIMO _____.

Answer on page 173.

WHAT THE CONSULTING DETECTIVE SAW
(PART I)

Study this picture of the crime scene for 1 minute, then turn the page.

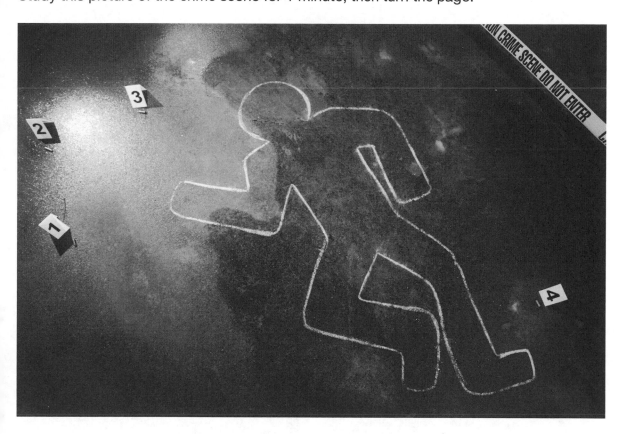

WHAT THE CONSULTING DETECTIVE SAW
(PART II)

(Do not read this until you have read the previous page!) Which image exactly matches the crime scene?

1

2

3

4

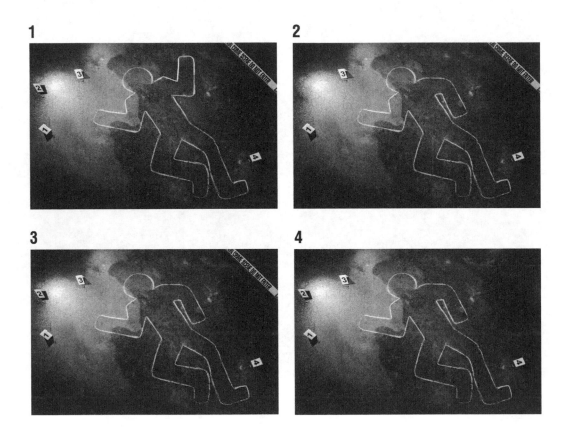

Answer on page 174.

EVERYBODY AND HIS BROTHER

Cryptograms are messages in substitution code. Break the code to read the message. For example, THE SMART CAT might become FVO QWGDF JGF if **F** is substituted for **T,** **V** for **H, O** for **E,** and so on.

PZLJH ZDHFILJADKH VKK AVPWKM LDK BPEJNI
MKLKZLFOK FY LDK 1962 EJOFK IDKHVJZR DJVEKI
PYM LDK MKPMVW YKZRVPZK. FY 1970, VKK AVP-
WKM P DJVEKI PCPFY—IDKHVJZR'I UHJLDKH EW-
ZHJBL, FY LDK EJOFK LDK AHFOPLK VFBK JB ID-
KHVJZR DJVEKI. DK DPM PVIJ AVPWKM IFH DKYHW
UPIRKHOFVVK FY PY KPHVFKH BFVE PMPALKM BHJE
LDK DJNYM JB LDK UPIRKHOFVVKI.

FOR HIS GENERATION

Cryptograms are messages in substitution code. Break the code to read the message. For example, THE SMART CAT might become FVO QWGDF JGF if **F** is substituted for **T,** **V** for **H, O** for **E,** and so on.

VFX VZ GQX LVEG ZDLVJE PVBGBDUDCE VZ QVCLXE
MDLX ZBVL IDENC BDGQIVFX NF GQX ZVBGNXE.
BDGQIVFX PCDUXS GQX SXGXMGNOX NF ZVJBGXXF
ZNCLE. XDBCNXB ZNCLE RXBX EXG NF ONMGVBNDF
GNLXE, RQNCX EVLX VZ GQX CDGXB NFEGDCCDGN-
VFE RXBX EXG NF GQX ZVBGNXE, RNGQ PCVGE
BXCDGXS GV GQX EXMVFS RVBCS RDB. GQXBX RDE
DCEV D BDSNV EXBNXE.

27   *Answers on page 174.*

THE EMPTY HOUSE

Each word or phrase in all capitals in the Sherlock Holmes quotation below is contained within the group of letters. Words can be found horizontally, vertically, or diagonally. They may read either forward or backward.

"I am all right, but indeed, Holmes, I can hardly BELIEVE my eyes. Good heavens! to think that you—you of all men—should be standing in my study." Again I gripped him by the sleeve, and felt the thin, SINEWY arm beneath it. "Well, you're not a SPIRIT anyhow," said I. "My dear chap, I'm overjoyed to see you. Sit down, and tell me how you came ALIVE out of that DREADFUL CHASM."

He sat opposite to me, and lit a cigarette in his old, nonchalant manner. He was dressed in the SEEDY frockcoat of the BOOK MERCHANT, but the rest of that individual lay in a pile of white hair and old books upon the table. Holmes looked even THINNER and KEENER than of old, but there was a dead-white TINGE in his AQUILINE face which told me that his life recently had not been a healthy one.

"I am glad to STRETCH myself, Watson," said he. "It is no joke when a tall man has to take a foot off his STATURE for several hours on end."

```
S  R  B  J  C  J  H  A  Q  U  I  L  I  N  E
N  P  D  J  H  C  B  L  K  D  Q  G  H  P  R
L  Z  T  T  T  G  D  Q  I  M  T  I  O  M  M
H  E  K  E  T  O  K  H  J  Q  H  I  S  E  P
A  H  R  E  S  J  B  F  Y  N  M  A  N  K  Y
V  T  H  T  I  R  I  P  S  H  H  K  K  G  B
S  X  N  T  N  K  M  L  A  C  L  W  I  O  E
H  X  O  T  E  M  D  F  L  E  A  C  L  K  L
V  W  I  E  W  L  I  U  M  F  T  L  R  K  I
S  P  N  J  Y  D  F  J  P  W  W  U  I  C  E
H  E  E  B  M  D  P  R  Y  D  E  E  S  V  V
R  E  T  N  A  H  C  R  E  M  K  O  O  B  E
T  K  U  E  T  H  I  N  N  E  R  H  S  L  Q
F  V  R  H  M  F  A  R  N  P  V  A  W  X  U
H  D  A  J  U  S  A  H  S  T  A  T  U  R  E
```

Answers on page 174.

CELEBRATING SHERLOCK

Cryptograms are messages in substitution code. Break the code to read the message. For example, THE SMART CAT might become FVO QWGDF JGF if **F** is substituted for **T, V** for **H, O** for **E,** and so on.

NMZ JDYZK LNKZZN LNFG FE NMZ AFEVFE OEVZKHK-FOEV MDL NRAZL NMDN LMFS NMZ LRAMFOZNNZ FC NMZ BFLN CDBFOL (RC CRPNRFEDA) KZLRVZEN FC NMDN LNKZZN. EZDKBW RL D BOLZOB VZQFNZV NF NMZ BDE DEV MRL SFKY.

CRACK THE PASSWORD

A detective has found a memory aid that the criminal left behind, a list of coded passwords. The detective knows that the criminal likes to scramble each password, then remove the same letter from each word. Can you figure out the missing letter and unscramble each word in this set to reveal the passwords?

MENTOR

PIANOS

REPEAL

CRUELLY

Answers on page 174.

WHAT WENT MISSING? (PART I)

The consulting detective met her client on Wednesday, and was told that some old family documents were hidden somewhere in the room. This was the room in which they met. Examine the room, then turn the page.

WHAT WENT MISSING? (PART II)

On Friday, the consulting detective was called back because her client had disappeared. The consulting detective noted that something else had gone missing. From memory, can you work out what went missing?

Answer on page 175.

WHAT THE CONSULTING DETECTIVE SAW
(PART I)

Study this picture of the crime scene for 1 minute, then turn the page.

WHAT THE CONSULTING DETECTIVE SAW (PART II)

(Do not read this until you have read the previous page!) Which image exactly matches the crime scene?

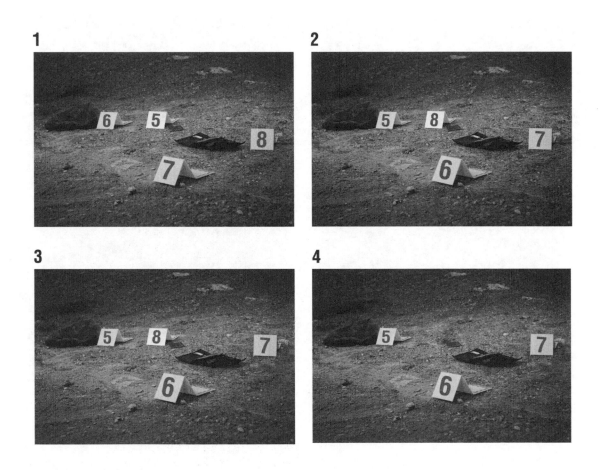

1

2

3

4

Answer on page 175.

TRACKING THE HOUND OF THE BASKERVILLES

Complete each quote from "The Hound of the Baskervilles" with one of the choices.

1. "A cast of your _____, sir, until the original is available, would be an ornament to any anthropological museum."

    A. teeth

    B. skull

    C. fingers

2. "The detection of _____ is one of the most elementary branches of knowledge to the special expert in crime, though I confess that once when I was very young I confused the "Leeds Mercury" with the "Western Morning News."

    A. types

    B. footprints

    C. newspaper clippings

3. "There is nothing more _____ than a case where everything goes against you."

    A. aggravating

    B. stimulating

    C. wonderful

4. "The world is full of _____ things which nobody by any chance ever observes."

    A. elementary

    B. mysterious

    C. obvious

5. "The past and the present are within the field of my _____, but what a man may do in the future is a hard question to answer."

    A. deductions

    B. inquiry

    C. observations

          Answers on page 175.

PASSING BAD CHECKS

Someone has been writing forged checks that have been bouncing all over San Pedro County! Four such checks have been reported so far, each in a different store and in a different town. None of the checks were for the same amount, and no two checks were written on the same day. Help Detective Punderson collect evidence by matching all four bad checks to the store and town in which they were used, and determining the date and total amount of each forged check.

1. Of the two checks written before October 8th, one was for $125.12 and the other was used in Georgetown.

2. The most expensive check was written eight days before the one used in Appleton.

3. The bad check passed at David's Deli was for either $125.12 or $35.15.

4. The check used in Georgetown was written four days before the one used at the Quick-Stop, and sometime after the one used at Carpet City.

5. The check for $52.89 was written 4 days before the one for $35.15.

6. The check passed in Lincoln was written sometime after the one for $125.12.

	Stores				Towns				Amounts			
	Carpet City	David's Deli	Quick-Stop	Well Mart	Appleton	Georgetown	Lincoln	Rio Pondo	$35.15	$52.89	$85.50	$125.12
Dates October 2												
October 6												
October 10												
October 14												
Amounts $35.15												
$52.89												
$85.50												
$125.12												
Towns Appleton												
Georgetown												
Lincoln												
Rio Pondo												

Dates	Stores	Towns	Amounts
October 2			
October 6			
October 10			
October 14			

Answers on page 175.

THE WOMEN OF SHERLOCK HOLMES

Every name listed is contained within the group of letters. Names can be found in a straight line horizontally, vertically, or diagonally. They may be read either forward or backward.

BERYL STAPLETON

EFFIE MUNRO

ELSIE PATRICK

EMILIA LUCCA

ELIZA BARRYMORE

EVA BLACKWELL

FRANCES CARFAX

HATTY DORAN

HELEN STONER

IRENE ADLER

LUCY FERRIER

MARY MORSTAN

MARY SUTHERLAND

NANCY BARCLAY

SUSAN CUSHING

VIOLET HUNTER

VIOLET SMITH

```
X A F R A C S E C N A R F F I
M A R Y S U T H E R L A N D F
Y A L C R A B Y C N A N K Z K
S U S A N C U S H I N G U C H
A K R E T N U H T E L O I V T
A Y L E F F I E M U N R O I I
B H M A R Y M O R S T A N R M
V H A T T Y D O R A N F R E S
B E R Y L S T A P L E T O N T
V B L U C Y F E R R I E R E E
A C C U L A I L I M E U C A L
H E L E N S T O N E R E N D O
E V A B L A C K W E L L T L I
S O T E C K O D E P E T Q E V
X E L I Z A B A R R Y M O R E
```

Answers on page 175.

A "CLERKS SHOO HELM" ANAGRAM

Below is a quotation from a Sherlock Holmes story. Fill in the blanks in each sentence with a word that is an anagram (rearrangement) of the capitalized word(s).

BONUS: Name the Sherlock Holmes adventure from which this quotation is drawn.

"My dear fellow," said Sherlock Holmes as we sat on either side of the fire in his GOLD SIGN _____ at Baker Street, "life is FILE IN TINY _____ stranger than anything which the mind of man could VET INN _____. We would not dare to NICE COVE _____ the things which are really mere CAMP MONOCLES _____ of existence. If we could fly out of that DIN WOW _____ hand in hand, hover over this great city, gently ME OVER _____ the roofs, and peep in at the queer things which are going on, the strange COINED SCENIC _____, the plannings, the cross-purposes, the FOWLED URN _____ chains of events, working through SO TANGERINE _____, and leading to the most outré results, it would make all fiction with its conventionalities and FREE NOSE _____ con-clusions most stale and FLAB ERUPTION _____."

Answers on page 175.

WHAT WENT MISSING? (PART I)

The consulting detective met his client on Thursday, and was told that some old family documents were hidden somewhere in the room. This was the room in which they met. Examine the room, then turn the page.

WHAT WENT MISSING? (PART II)

On Friday, the consulting detective was called back because his client had disappeared. The consulting detective noted that something else had gone missing. From memory, can you work out what went missing?

Answer on page 176.

WHAT THE CONSULTING DETECTIVE SAW
(PART I)

Study this picture of the crime scene for 1 minute, then turn the page.

WHAT THE CONSULTING DETECTIVE SAW (PART II)

(Do not read this until you have read the previous page!) Which image exactly matches the crime scene?

1

2

3

4

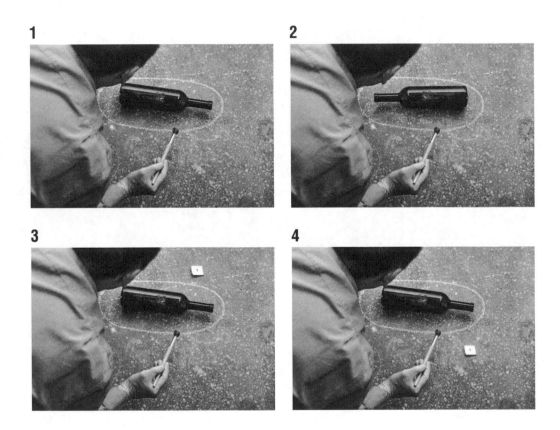

Answer on page 176.

INTERCEPTION

You've intercepted a message that is meant to reveal a location for an upcoming meeting between two criminal masterminds. The only problem is, the message shows many place names. Can you figure out the right location?

ICELAND

LESOTHO

TONGA

INDIA

COMOROS

BENIN

Answer on page 176.

THE ESCAPE ARTIST

Marco Antonini, an infamous jewel thief, has made a name for himself over the years as something of an escape artist. He's broken his way out of five different prisons, each in a different state, and each using a different method (such as a tunnel or a guard's uniform). Using only the clues below, match each of his successful escape attempts to the correct year, jail, and state, and determine the method he used during each.

1. Marco broke out of Tulveride prison 4 years after he escaped from Middle Fork.

2. His most recent escape, the Pennington break-out, and the escape where he wore a guard's uniform occurred in three different states.

3. The 2009 escape didn't involve wire cutters.

4. Marco used a guard's uniform as a disguise 4 years after he broke out of Middle Fork prison.

5. The Alabama escape was 12 years before the one in Virginia.

6. Marco broke out of Lexington prison 12 years after his Middle Fork escape.

7. Of the two break-outs where Marco used a rope and a guard's uniform, one was at Calahatchee prison and the other was in 2005.

8. A rope made out of bedsheets was all Marco needed to break out of the prison in Colorado.

9. Marco wasn't in Montana in 2005, and he used neither wire cutters nor a tunnel for his Virginia escape.

	Prisons					States					Methods				
	Calahatchee	Lexington	Middle Fork	Pennington	Tulveride	Alabama	Colorado	Idaho	Montana	Virginia	Ladder	Rope	Tunnel	Uniform	Wire cutters
Years 2001															
2005															
2009															
2013															
2017															
Methods Ladder															
Rope															
Tunnel															
Uniform															
Wire cutters															
States Alabama															
Colorado															
Idaho															
Montana															
Virginia															

Years	Prisons	States	Methods
2001			
2005			
2009			
2013			
2017			

47

Answers on page 176.

FAMOUS FIRST LINES

How well do you know the Holmes canon? Match the first line of each story to the story's title.

1. When I glance over my notes and records of the Sherlock Holmes cases between the years '82 and '90, I am faced by so many which present strange and interesting features that it is no easy matter to know which to choose and which to leave.

2. Mrs. Hudson, the landlady of Sherlock Holmes, was a long-suffering woman.

3. It was no very unusual thing for Mr. Lestrade, of Scotland Yard, to look in upon us of an evening, and his visits were welcome to Sherlock Holmes, for they enabled him to keep in touch with all that was going on at the police headquarters.

4. "I am afraid, Watson, that I shall have to go," said Holmes, as we sat down together to our breakfast one morning.

5. "I have some papers here," said my friend Sherlock Holmes, as we sat one winter's night on either side of the fire, "which I really think, Watson, that it would be worth your while to glance over."

A. The Adventure of Silver Blaze

B. The Five Orange Pips

C. The Adventure of the "Gloria Scott"

D. The Adventure of the Dying Detective

E. The Adventure of the Six Napoleons

Answers on page 176.

FINGERPRINT MATCH

There are 8 sets of fingerprints. Find each match.

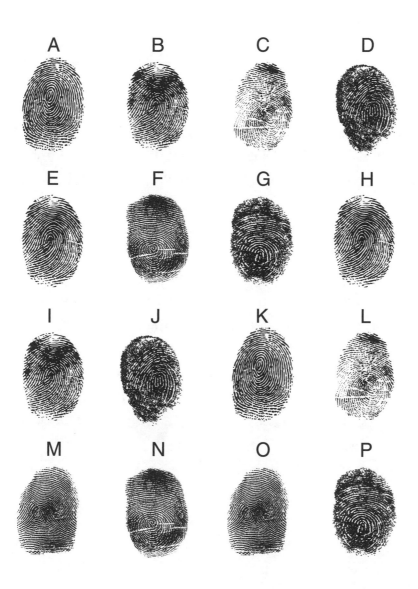

Answers on page 176.

THE "GLORIA SCOTT"

Each word or phrase in all capitals in the Sherlock Holmes quotation below is contained within the group of letters. Words can be found horizontally, vertically, or diagonally. They may read either forward or backward.

"You never heard me talk of VICTOR TREVOR?" he asked. "He was the only FRIEND I made during the two years I was at COLLEGE. I was never a very SOCIABLE fellow, Watson, always rather fond of MOPING in my rooms and working out my own little METHODS of thought, so that I never mixed much with the men of my year. Bar FENCING and BOXING I had few athletic tastes, and then my line of STUDY was quite distinct from that of the other FELLOWS, so that we had no points of contact at all. Trevor was the only man I knew, and that only through the ACCIDENT of his BULL TERRIER freezing on to my ANKLE one morning as I went down to CHAPEL.

"It was a PROSAIC way of forming a friendship, but it was effective. I was laid by the heels for ten days, but Trevor used to come in to INQUIRE after me. At first it was only a minute's chat, but soon his VISITS lengthened, and before the end of the term we were close friends. He was a hearty, full-blooded fellow, full of spirits and energy, the very OPPOSITE to me in most respects, but we had some subjects in common, and it was a bond of UNION when I found that he was as friendless as I. Finally, he invited me down to his father's place at Donnithorpe, in Norfolk, and I accepted his HOSPITALITY for a month of the long VACATION."

```
I  N  P  Q  G  P  P  V  N  O  M  J  E  L  L
G  T  N  E  D  I  C  C  A  A  B  C  E  Y  B
Y  T  I  L  A  T  I  P  S  O  H  P  I  U  V
F  E  N  C  I  N  G  N  X  T  A  P  L  K  A
L  I  Q  R  L  O  Z  I  H  H  I  L  T  H  C
R  G  U  U  X  Z  N  S  C  C  T  S  H  Y  A
I  F  I  M  Z  G  V  F  Z  E  S  U  I  W  T
C  E  R  O  V  E  R  T  R  O  T  C  I  V  I
O  L  E  P  T  I  U  R  C  T  Z  S  Y  G  O
L  L  R  I  E  S  I  I  V  D  Y  I  U  B  N
L  O  Z  N  Q  E  A  H  U  D  A  N  K  L  E
E  W  D  G  R  B  O  Z  U  U  N  I  O  N  E
G  S  H  C  L  M  E  T  H  O  D  S  Y  W  T
E  Q  V  E  F  J  S  P  R  O  S  A  I  C  Z
M  E  T  I  S  O  P  P  O  D  C  S  V  H  G
```

Answers on page 176.

A SURPRISING VIEWPOINT

Cryptograms are messages in substitution code. Break the code to read the message. For example, THE SMART CAT might become FVO QWGDF JGF if **F** is substituted for **T**, **V** for **H**, **O** for **E**, and so on.

BONUS: Who is the speaker, and which story is the source of the quote?

"R FCAKRHJI MPBM B ZBA'K DIBRA CIRNRABXXW RK XRVJ B XRMMXJ JZEMW BMMRF, BAH WCO PBQJ MC KMCFV RM SRMP KOFP LOIARMOIJ BK WCO FPCCKJ. B LCCX MBVJK RA BXX MPJ XOZDJI CL JQIJW KCIM MPBM PJ FCZJK BFICKK, KC MPBM MPJ VACSXJHNJ SPRFP ZRNPM DJ OKJLOX MC PRZ NJMK FICSHJH COM, CI BM DJKM RK TOZDXJH OE SRMP B XCM CL CMPJI MPRANK KC MPBM PJ PBK B HRLLRFOXMW RA XBWRAN PRK PBAHK OECA RM. ACS MPJ KVRX-LOX SCIVZBA RK QJIW FBIJLOX RAHJJH BK MC SPBM PJ MBVJK RAMC PRK DIBRA-BMMRF. PJ SRXX PBQJ ACMPRAN DOM MPJ MCCXK SPRFP ZBW PJXE PRZ RA HCRAN PRK SCIV, DOM CL MPJKJ PJ PBK B XBINJ BKKCIMZJAM, BAH BXX RA MPJ ZCKM EJILJFM CIHJI. RM RK B ZRKMBVJ MC MPRAV MPBM MPBM XRM-MXJ ICCZ PBK JXBKMRF SBXXK BAH FBA HRKMJAH MC BAW JUMJAM. HJEJAH OECA RM MPJIJ FCZJK B MRZJ SPJA LCI JQIJW BHHRMRCA CL VACSXJHNJ WCO LCINJM KCZJMPRAN MPBM WCO VAJS DJLCIJ. RM RK CL MPJ PRNPJKM RZECIMBAFJ, MPJIJLCIJ, ACM MC PBQJ OKJXJKK LBFMK JXDCSRAN COM MPJ OKJLOX CAJK."

                                                    Answers on page 177.

WHAT WENT MISSING? (PART I)

The consulting detective visited the dressing room of the actress who had received threats. Examine the objects, then turn the page.

WHAT WENT MISSING? (PART II)

Overnight, the actress got sick from poison and was rushed to the hospital! The consulting detective noted something missing from her dressing room and suspected it had contained the poison. From memory, can you work out what went missing?

Answer on page 177.

IN CAP AND CAPE

Cryptograms are messages in substitution code. Break the code to read the message. For example, THE SMART CAT might become FVO QWGDF JGF if **F** is substituted for **T**, **V** for **H**, **O** for **E**, and so on.

EGVKA'H HLGFBAH SAFA HAFBUKBWAE BP U XUZU-WBPA IUKKAE LQA HLFUPE, UPE UIIGXCUPBAE OV BKKNHLFULBGPH IFAULAE OV HBEPAV CUZAL. LQA BEAU LQUL QGKXAH SGFA U EAAFHLUKMAF IUC UPE UP BPRAFPAHH IUCA IGXAH PGL EBFAILKV JFGX EGVKA ONL JFGX CUZAL'H BKKNHLFULBGPH. CUZAL QUE LSG OFGLQAFH, OGLQ BKKNHLFULGFH; OV GPA UIIGNPL, OFGLQAF SUKLAF SUH GFBZBPUKKV BPLAPEAE LG EG LQA JBFHL BKKNHLFULBGPH, ONL LQA CNOKBHQAFH HAPL LQA KALLAF LG HBEPAV BPHLAUE.

Answers on page 177.

AN ENDURING TRAIT

Cryptograms are messages in substitution code. Break the code to read the message. For example, THE SMART CAT might become FVO QWGDF JGF if **F** is substituted for **T**, **V** for **H**, **O** for **E**, and so on.

NEP ZPNPVNORP'L LOFAJNQKP VJBJGJLE DODP
TJL DCDQBJKOYPZ GW TOBBOJM FOBBPNNP, TEC
DBJWPZ ECBMPL CA LNJFP OA NEP BJNP 1800L
JAZ PJKBW 1900L. LOZAPW DJFPN'L OBBQLNKJNO-
CAL LECTPZ NEP LBPQNE TONE J LNKJOFEN DODP,
GQN FOBBPNNP QLPZ J VQKRW VJBJGJLE DODP,
J ZPNJOB NEJN BJLNPZ OA NEP ZPVJZPL NEJN
HCBBCTPZ.

CRACK THE PASSWORD

A detective has found a memory aid that the criminal left behind, a list of coded passwords. The detective knows that the criminal likes to scramble each password, then remove the same letter from each word. Can you figure out the missing letter and unscramble each word in this set to reveal the passwords?

AROMA

TRANCE

FOAMING

AMICUS

Answers on page 177.

WHAT WENT MISSING? (PART I)

The consulting detective visited the study of a writer who had received mysterious notes. Examine the objects on the writer's desk, then turn the page.

WHAT WENT MISSING? (PART II)

The next day, the writer was attacked! The butler rushed in to see a mysterious assailant who fled, and the butler got the writer to the hopsital. From the wounds, the writer was stabbed by something sharp, but the assailant fled with the weapon. The consulting detective visited the scene and noted the absence of an object that was the likely weapon. From memory, can you work out what went missing?

Answer on page 178.

A "OH SHELL MOCKERS" ANAGRAM

Below is a quotation from a Sherlock Holmes story. Fill in the blanks in each sentence with a word that is an anagram (rearrangement) of the capitalized word(s).

BONUS: Name the Sherlock Holmes adventure from which this quotation is drawn.

"MANICURIST TALC _____ VICE NEED _____ is a very tricky thing," answered Holmes thoughtfully. "It may seem to point very TAG SHIRT _____ to one thing, but if you shift your own point of view a little, you may find it pointing in an equally MORONIC IMPUGNS _____ manner to something entirely different. It must be confessed, however, that the case looks EXCEL DYEING _____ grave against the young man, and it is very possible that he is indeed the CURT LIP _____. There are several people in the neighbourhood, however, and among them Miss Turner, the daughter of the neighbouring DAWN LONER _____, who believe in his NICE NONCE _____, and who have EARNED IT _____ Lestrade, whom you may recollect in connection with the Study in CARTELS _____, to work out the case in his interest. Lestrade, being rather puzzled, has FREED ERR _____ the case to me, and hence it is that two middle-aged TEN LEGMEN _____ are flying WARTS WED _____ at fifty miles an hour instead of quietly DIGS TINGE _____ their STAB FAKERS _____ at home."

Answers on page 178.

THE MUSGRAVE RITUAL

Each word or phrase in all capitals in the Sherlock Holmes quotation below is contained within the group of letters. Words can be found horizontally, vertically, or diagonally. They may read either forward or backward.

Our CHAMBERS were always full of CHEMICALS and of criminal RELICS which had a way of wandering into unlikely positions, and of turning up in the BUTTER-DISH or in even less desirable places. But his PAPERS were my great CRUX. He had a horror of destroying DOCUMENTS, especially those which were connected with his past CASES, and yet it was only once in every year or two that he would MUSTER energy to DOCKET and arrange them; for, as I have mentioned somewhere in these incoherent MEMOIRS, the OUTBURSTS of passionate ENERGY when he performed the remarkable feats with which his name is associated were followed by reactions of LETHARGY during which he would lie about with his VIOLIN and his books, hardly moving save from the SOFA to the table. Thus month after month his papers ACCUMULATED, until every corner of the room was stacked with BUNDLES of manuscript which were on no account to be BURNED, and which could not be put away save by their OWNER.

```
D E B P Y A U A F O S N G T Z
X R I U R E T S U M W Y G B J
U N D O N A E A P F Z G P U J
R R I O H D O U T B U R S T S
C F S L C J L S R E P A P T S
B B E R O K I E G Y S H J E T
M W R M I I E S S G L T C R N
E L Z D X O V T E R A E H D E
R E L I C S M B K E C L N I M
R C U D O S U E W N I U N S U
E A I S C R V R M E M T Y H C
N S Y N N C H A M B E R S J O
W E Z E A X T N Q D H Q N E D
O S D H Z P G P Y O C A S T A
C D E T A L U M U C C A X H T
```

Answers on page 178.

THE SUSPECT LIST

There's been a murder at the Forsyth Mansion! It happened sometime last evening during a fancy dinner party, and five guests who were present at the time are now considered possible suspects. Each has a different profession and is from a different town. None of the five men are the same age. Help the police sort out their investigation by matching each suspect to his age, profession, and home town.

1. Albert isn't the oldest of the five men.

2. The Flagstaff native is 3 years older than the suspect from Midvale (who isn't the dentist), and six years younger than the architect.

3. The engineer is older than Vincent.

4. Nicholas, who is from Billings, is 3 years older than Michael. Of the two of them, one is 26 years old and the other is the tennis pro.

5. The dentist isn't from Flagstaff.

6. Dennis lives in downtown San Pedro.

Logic Grid

	Suspects					Professions					Towns				
	Albert	Dennis	Michael	Nicholas	Vincent	Architect	Dentist	Engineer	Lawyer	Tennis pro	Billings	Flagstaff	Midvale	San Pedro	Tulverton
Ages 23															
26															
29															
32															
35															
Towns Billings										
Flagstaff										
Midvale										
San Pedro										
Tulverton										
Professions Architect					
Dentist					
Engineer					
Lawyer					
Tennis pro					

Ages	Suspects	Professions	Towns
23			
26			
29			
32			
35			

Answers on page 178.

INTERCEPTION

You've intercepted a message that is meant to reveal a location for an upcoming meeting between two criminal masterminds. The only problem is, the message shows many place names. Can you figure out the right location?

ABUJA

BUDAPEST

ACCRA

DHAKA

JAKARTA

TRIPOLI

SEOUL

ASTANA

ATHENS

Answer on page 178.

WHAT THE CONSULTING DETECTIVE SAW
(PART I)

Study this picture of the crime scene for 1 minute, then turn the page.

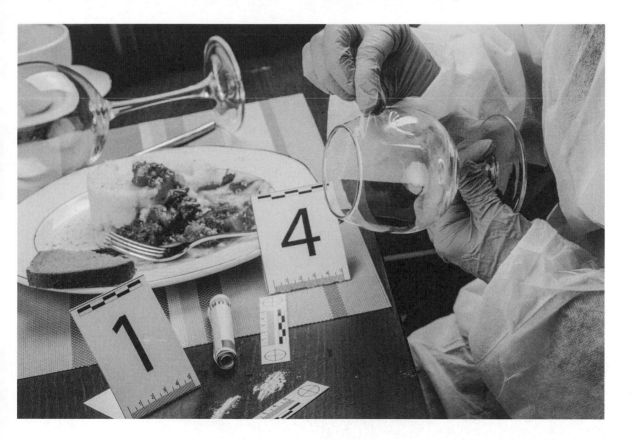

WHAT THE CONSULTING DETECTIVE SAW
(PART II)

(Do not read this until you have read the previous page!)

1. How many numbered placards are found on the table?

____ One, numbered 1

____ Two, numbered 1 and 2

____ Two, numbered 1 and 4

2. The crime scene investigator is holding this object to examine it.

____ Wineglass

____ Teacup

____ Fork

3. This utensil is resting on the plate.

____ Spoon

____ Fork

____ Butter knife

4. The food on the plate includes a slice of bread.

____ True

____ False

5. A wineglass had been knocked over.

____ True

____ False

Answers on page 179.

RENTAL AGREEMENTS

Cryptograms are messages in substitution code. Break the code to read the message. For example, THE SMART CAT might become FVO QWGDF JGF if **F** is substituted for **T**, **V** for **H**, **O** for **E**, and so on.

BONUS QUESTION: Who is described in the quote? Which story is the source of the quote?

EFN FEMW SHL CBJ KTJLN-KMFFJ KMHN TER-
HZBZ HN HMM CFQJL PW NCJFEOL FK LTEOQMHJ
HEZ FKNBE QEZBLTJHPMB UCHJHUNBJL PQN CBJ
JBAHJYHPMB MFZOBJ LCFSBZ HE BUUBENJTUTNW
HEZ TJJBOQMHJTNW TE CTL MTKB SCTUC AQLN
CHRB LFJBMW NJTBZ CBJ GHNTBEUB. CTL TEU-
JBZTPMB QENTZTEBLL, CTL HZZTUNTFE NF AQLTU
HN LNJHEOB CFQJL, CTL FUUHLTFEHM JBRFMRBJ
GJHUNTUB STNCTE ZFFJL, CTL SBTJZ HEZ FKNBE
AHMFZFJFQL LUTBENTKTU BVGBJTABENL, HEZ NCB
HNAFLGCBJB FK RTFMBEUB HEZ ZHEOBJ SCTUC
CQEO HJFQEZ CTA AHZB CTA NCB RBJW SFJLN NBE-
HEN TE MFEZFE. FE NCB FNCBJ CHEZ, CTL GHWA-
BENL SBJB GJTEUBMW.

67 Answers on page 179.

TELEPHONE RECORDS

A local artist named George Wilson has been reported missing. The police have learned that five calls were made from his cell phone on the night he disappeared. None of the five calls were to the same number, and each of them lasted for a different length of time. Using only the clues below, help sort out the information by matching each call to its owner, number, and time, and determine the length of each phone call.

1. Mitchell's phone number doesn't start with "368".

2. The longest phone call was placed five minutes before George dialed 731-9262, and sometime before he called Sarah.

3. Charlie's number is 447-6995.

4. The 48-second phone call was to either Kerry or whoever has the phone number starting with "731".

5. George dialed 592-0021 15 minutes after the 22-second phone call.

6. Whoever received the 3-minute phone call, the person George called at 2:07am, and Vicky are three different people.

7. George called Vicky sometime before 2:10am.

8. Of the two calls placed before 2:00am, one lasted for 3 minutes and the other was to the "239" number.

9. Kerry's home phone number is 239-4827.

10. The 2:07am call didn't last for exactly a minute and a half.

		Charlie	Kerry	Mitchell	Sarah	Vicky	239-4827	368-7841	447-6995	592-0021	731-9262	22 seconds	35 seconds	48 seconds	1.5 minutes	3 minutes
		People					**Numbers**					**Lengths**				
Times	1:52am															
	1:57am															
	2:02am															
	2:07am															
	2:12am															
Lengths	22 seconds															
	35 seconds															
	48 seconds															
	1.5 minutes															
	3 minutes															
Numbers	239-4827															
	368-7841															
	447-6995															
	592-0021															
	731-9262															

Times	People	Numbers	Lengths
1:52am			
1:57am			
2:02am			
2:07am			
2:12am			

Answers on page 179.

THE ADVENTURE OF THE RESIDENT PATIENT

Each word or phrase in all capitals in the Sherlock Holmes quotation below is contained within the group of letters. Words can be found horizontally, vertically, or diagonally. They may read either forward or backward.

In glancing over the somewhat INCOHERENT series of Memoirs with which I have ENDEAVORED to ILLUSTRATE a few of the mental PECULIARITIES of my friend Mr. Sherlock Holmes, I have been struck by the difficulty which I have experienced in picking out EXAMPLES which shall in every way answer my PURPOSE. For in those cases in which Holmes has performed some TOUR DE FORCE of analytical REASONING, and has demonstrated the VALUE of his peculiar methods of INVESTIGATION, the facts themselves have often been so SLIGHT or so COMMONPLACE that I could not feel JUSTIFIED in laying them before the PUBLIC. On the other hand, it has frequently happened that he has been concerned in some RESEARCH where the facts have been of the most remarkable and DRAMATIC character, but where the share which he has himself taken in determining their causes has been less PRONOUNCED than I, as his BIOGRAPHER, could wish. The small matter which I have CHRONICLED under the heading of "A Study in Scarlet," and that other later one connected with the loss of the Gloria Scott, may serve as examples of this SCYLLA and CHARYBDIS which are forever threatening the HISTORIAN.

```
B Z S E L P M A X E E E L X K W N
V I P U U E C A L P N O M M O C K
R L S L X N L I N C O H E R E N T
X L R A J U S T I F I E D T Y F B
E U E V K M D L K H K A J O T F I
M S A P N J B E L Z S M E U H P O
S T S P Q U A L L Y C S E R G U G
Y R O A P N V Q F C F P U D I R R
U A N E U J G S F O I X O E L P A
R T I C I T A M A R D N G F S O P
E E N L I T G Q L U N I O O L S H
S A G M M D E C N U O N O R P E E
E N D E A V O R E D P O T C H O R
A S I D B Y R A H C U M Q E U C P
R S J Q N O I T A G I T S E V N I
C N A I R O T S I H D C C T R K B
H P E C U L I A R I T I E S U Y O
```

Answers on page 179.

A "LOCK HELM HORSES" ANAGRAM

Below is a quotation from a Sherlock Holmes story. Fill in the blanks in each sentence with a word that is an anagram (rearrangement) of the capitalized word(s).

BONUS: Name the Sherlock Holmes adventure from which this quotation is drawn.

He was a man of about fifty, tall, LOP TRY _____, and imposing, with a massive, strongly marked face and a DANCING MOM _____ figure. He was dressed in a sombre yet rich style, in black CRAFT COOK _____, shining hat, neat brown TRIAGES _____, and well-cut pearl-grey ORE RUSTS _____. Yet his actions were in absurd contrast to the TIDYING _____ of his dress and features, for he was running hard, with CACAO LIONS _____ little springs, such as a weary man gives who is little CACTUS DEMO _____ to set any tax upon his legs. As he ran he jerked his hands up and down, waggled his head, and HERD WIT _____ his face into the most extraordinary CITRON SNOOT _____.

Answers on page 180.

WHAT WENT MISSING? (PART I)

The consulting detective was at a house party. What did she see in the garden shed? Examine the objects, then turn the page.

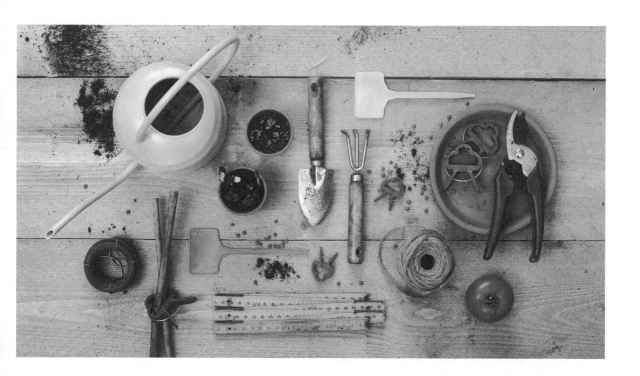

WHAT WENT MISSING? (PART II)

There was a murder at the house party! The consulting detective immediately spotted that one object went missing, and that object was probably the murder weapon. From memory, can you work out what went missing?

Answer on page 180.

A SEEKER OF TRUTH

Cryptograms are messages in substitution code. Break the code to read the message. For example, THE SMART CAT might become FVO QWGDF JGF if **F** is substituted for **T, V** for **H, O** for **E,** and so on.

PA KNV 1930J, BVAHFDP OIPKVI JNFIFQPAQL BFAQXCE-FQNXFX PAKICQLTVQ F TNFIFTKVI AFSVQ BXCSWVJN BFWJNP, ONC JCDMVQ SXJKVIPVJ BLK EIVZVIIVQ KNV KVIS "KILKN-JVVWVI" KC QVKVTKPMV. KNV TNFIFTKVI FEEVFIVQ PA 32 JKCIPVJ PA KNV QVTFQVJ KNFK ZCD-DCOVQ, FAQ PAJEPIVQ F KVDVMPJPCA JNCO FAQ JVM-VIFD SCMPVJ. NV'J BVVA TFDDVQ "KNV PAQPFA JNVIDC-TW NCDSVJ."

CRACK THE PASSWORD

A detective has found a memory aid that the criminal left behind, a list of coded passwords. The detective knows that the criminal likes to scramble each password, then remove the same letter from each word. Can you figure out the missing letter and unscramble each word in this set to reveal the passwords?

PARCEL

RESEATED

PILFER

UNIT

Answers on page 180.

GRAVE ROBBERIES

The state police have been called in to investigate a series of bizarre grave robberies perpetrated in five different cemeteries across Bolton County. Each occurred on a different date and at a different cemetery, none of which were in the same town. Only one grave was robbed in each cemetery. Using only the clues below, help the police solve this mystery by determining the date on which each of the five graves were robbed, as well as the cemetery and town in which each was located.

1. Of the March 20th incident and the one at Dinby Dale Cemetery, one was in Upperdale and the other involved the grave of Ed Lowder.

2. Pat Fowler was interred at Green Lawn Cemetery in Shell City.

3. Holden Bray's grave (which was in either Calvary Cape Cemetery or the cemetery in Verona) was robbed 8 days before the incident in Trenton.

4. Brad Beaudry's grave wasn't robbed on the night of March 20th.

5. Of the two robberies in Upperdale and Shell City, one was at Apple Pine Cemetery and the other was on March 28th.

6. Ed Lowder wasn't buried in Verona.

7. The cemetery in Upperdale was robbed sometime before the one in Wilmette.

		Cemeteries					Graves					Towns				
		Apple Pine	Box Grove	Calvary Cape	Dinby Dale	Green Lawn	Brad Beaudry	Ed Lowder	Holden Bray	Pat Fowler	Ruben Yates	Shell City	Trenton	Upperdale	Verona	Wilmette
Dates	March 12th															
	March 20th															
	March 28th															
	April 5th															
	April 13th															
Towns	Shell City															
	Trenton															
	Upperdale															
	Verona															
	Wilmette															
Graves	Brad Beaudry															
	Ed Lowder															
	Holden Bray															
	Pat Fowler															
	Ruben Yates															

Dates	Cemeteries	Graves	Towns
March 12th			
March 20th			
March 28th			
April 5th			
April 13th			

Answers on page 180.

FAMOUS LAST LINES

How well do you know the Holmes canon? Match the last line of each story to the story's title.

1. We did at last hear that somewhere far out in the Atlantic a shattered stern-post of a boat was seen swinging in the trough of a wave, with the letters "L. S." carved upon it, and that is all which we shall ever know of the fate of the "Lone Star."

2. "If you will have the goodness to touch the bell, Doctor, we will begin another investigation, in which, also a bird will be the chief feature."

3. "Watson," said he, "if it should ever strike you that I am getting a little over-confident in my powers, or giving less pains to a case than it deserves, kindly whisper 'Norbury' in my ear, and I shall be infinitely obliged to you."

4. And he stretched his long white hand up for it.

5. "I have a check for five hundred pounds which should be cashed early, for the drawer is quite capable of stopping it if he can."

A. The Adventure of the Yellow Face

B. The Sign of the Four

C. The Adventure of the Blue Carbuncle

D. The Adventure of the Five Orange Pips

E. His Last Bow

Answers on page 180.

DUALITY

Cryptograms are messages in substitution code. Break the code to read the message. For example, THE SMART CAT might become FVO QWGDF JGF if **F** is substituted for **T**, **V** for **H, O** for **E,** and so on.

XQOT QDJMHI EQPK BYQTKN EMYXKI, QON XQOT
EQPK BYQTKN RQJIMO — ZLJ ZHGJGIE QDJMH BQJH-
GDA XQDOKK RQI MOK MU JEK UKR JM BYQT ZMJE
HMYKI NLHGOV Q YMOV DQHKKH! EK BYQTKN JEK
DEQHQDJKH MU RQJIMO MBBMIGJK HMVKH XMMHK
QON DEHGIJMBEKH YKK. QON JM DQB GJ MUU, GO
1984, EK BYQTKN Q DEQHQDJKH MO JEK JKYKPGIG-
MO IEMR XQVOLX B.G. REM EQN Q NKYLIGMO JEQJ
EK RQI IEKHYMDA EMYXKI.

79

THE ADVENTURE OF THE GREEK INTERPRETER

Each word or phrase in all capitals in the Sherlock Holmes quotation below is contained within the group of letters. Words can be found horizontally, vertically, or diagonally. They may read either forward or backward.

"What is to me a means of LIVELIHOOD is to him the merest HOBBY of a DILETTANTE. He has an EXTRAORDINARY faculty for figures, and AUDITS the books in some of the GOVERNMENT departments. MYCROFT lodges in Pall Mall, and he walks round the corner into WHITEHALL every morning and back every evening. From year's end to year's end he takes no other exercise, and is seen nowhere else, except only in the DIOGENES CLUB, which is just opposite his rooms."

"I cannot recall the name."

"Very likely not. There are many men in London, you know, who, some from SHYNESS, some from MISANTHROPY, have no wish for the COMPANY of their fellows. Yet they are not AVERSE to comfortable chairs and the latest PERIODICALS. It is for the convenience of these that the Diogenes Club was started, and it now contains the most UNSOCIABLE and UNCLUBABLE men in town. No MEMBER is permitted to take the least notice of any other one. Save in the STRANGER'S ROOM, no talking is, under any circumstances, allowed, and three OFFENCES, if brought to the notice of the committee, render the talker liable to EXPULSION. My brother was one of the FOUNDERS, and I have myself found it a very SOOTHING atmosphere."

```
D Y W C U X H F S I T F O R C Y M
I R G G R Z O R L Y E Y M T M G Y
O A L V Y U B G A P A B E N O N N
G N I U N O S V C O A B T E O I A
E I V D L P E A I R U O N M R H P
N D E L F R C W D H D H A N S T M
E R L N S Z N H O T I V T R R O O
S O I E I E I I N T Y T E E O C
C A H Z P L F T R A S L E V G S K
L R O Y G B F E E S W H L O N D O
U T O W I A O H P I H T I G A H H
B X D I U B J A R M J Y D S R Y D
R E P J N U X L I W I O N E T B U
W A F K A L A L A K A U B E S B L
E L B A I C O S N U Y M L B S I U
K V C I E N F W V F E R Y I V S S
N O I S L U P X E M X Z D L N C K
```

81　　　　　　　　　　　　　　*Answers on page 181.*

A "MOCKS SHELL HERO" ANAGRAM

Below is a quotation from a Sherlock Holmes story. Fill in the blanks in each sentence with a word that is an anagram (rearrangement) of the capitalized word(s).

BONUS: Name the Sherlock Holmes adventure from which this quotation is drawn.

"Pshaw, my dear fellow, what do the public, the great BRAVEST NOUN _____ public, who could hardly tell a WE RAVE _____ by his tooth or a compositor by his left thumb, care about the finer shades of SAY SNAIL _____ and deduction! But, indeed, if you are VIRAL IT _____, I cannot blame you, for the days of the great cases are past. Man, or at least criminal man, has lost all SERENE TRIP _____ and IRON AGILITY _____. As to my own little practice, it seems to be TEE GARDENING _____ into an agency for recovering lost lead pencils and giving CAVE ID _____ to young ladies from boarding-schools. I think that I have touched bottom at last, however. This note I had this morning marks my zero-point, I fancy. Read it!" He tossed a RED CLUMP _____ letter across to me.

Answers on page 181.

WHAT WENT MISSING? (PART I)

At a client's house, the consulting detective saw many tools laid out. Study the objects, then turn the page.

WHAT WENT MISSING? (PART II)

The following day, a guest was knocked over the head when he interrupted a theft in progress. Whatever was used as a weapon was taken away. The consulting detective sees that one object was missing from the previous day. From memory, can you work out what went missing?

Answer on page 181.

ANOTHER RESIDENT OF BAKER STREET

Cryptograms are messages in substitution code. Break the code to read the message. For example, THE SMART CAT might become FVO QWGDF JGF if **F** is substituted for **T**, **V** for **H, O** for **E,** and so on.

XF HMN HNPNLXEXYF EMYO MYIEN, HMN HXHPN
WMBDBWHND, RDNRYDU MYIEN, OBE JBDHPU XFE-
JXDNZ QU BFZ MBE TBFU WMBDBWHNDXEHXWE XF
WYTTYF OXHM HMN GXWHXYFBP ZNHNWHXLN NLNF
HMYIRM HMN TUEHNDXNE MN EYPLNZ ONDN TNZX-
WBP XFEHNBZ YG WDXTXFBP. EMYDN, HMN EMYO'E
WDNBHYD, OBE B QXR GBF. MYIEN, PXKN MXE JDN-
ZNWNEEYD, OBE XDBEWXQPN, MBZ B WYTJBFXYF
(CBTNE OXPEYF XFEHNBZ YG CYMF OBHEYF), BFZ
NLNF PXLNZ YF QBKND EHDNNH! HMN FBTNE MYIEN,
XF GBWH, EYIFZE PXKN "MYTNE," B MYTYFUT YG
HMN ZNHNWHXLN'E FBTN.

Answers on page 182.

WITNESS STATEMENTS

There was a break-in at Sal's jewelry store last night! Police have interviewed five people who claimed to have witnessed the theft, but their stories vary quite a bit. Help the police sort out their statements by matching each witness report to the correct height and weight of the person they saw, and the type of car in which they made their getaway.

1. Of the person Gerald saw and the 190-pound suspect, one was 5'2" and the other drove a Nissan.

2. The man Russell saw was 3 inches shorter than whoever was driving the Toyota, and 6 inches shorter than the 135-pound suspect.

3. Yolanda's suspect was either 5'2" or 5'8" tall.

4. The 190-pound suspect was nine inches shorter than whoever was driving the Mazda.

5. The man driving the Honda appeared to be 5'8" tall.

6. Angela's suspect wasn't 5'5" tall or 160 pounds.

7. The 145-pound suspect wasn't 5'11", and didn't drive the Nissan.

	Witnesses					Weights					Cars				
	Angela S.	Gerald F.	Russell T.	Sarah M.	Yolanda V.	135 lbs	145 lbs	160 lbs	190 lbs	225 lbs	Chevrolet	Honda	Mazda	Nissan	Toyota
Heights 5' 2"															
5' 5"															
5' 8"															
5' 11"															
6' 2"															
Cars Chevrolet															
Honda															
Mazda															
Nissan															
Toyota															
Weights 135 lbs															
145 lbs															
160 lbs															
190 lbs															
225 lbs															

Heights	Witnesses	Weights	Cars
5' 2"			
5' 5"			
5' 8"			
5' 11"			
6' 2"			

Answers on page 182.

FINGERPRINT MATCH

Find the matching fingerprint(s). There may be more than one.

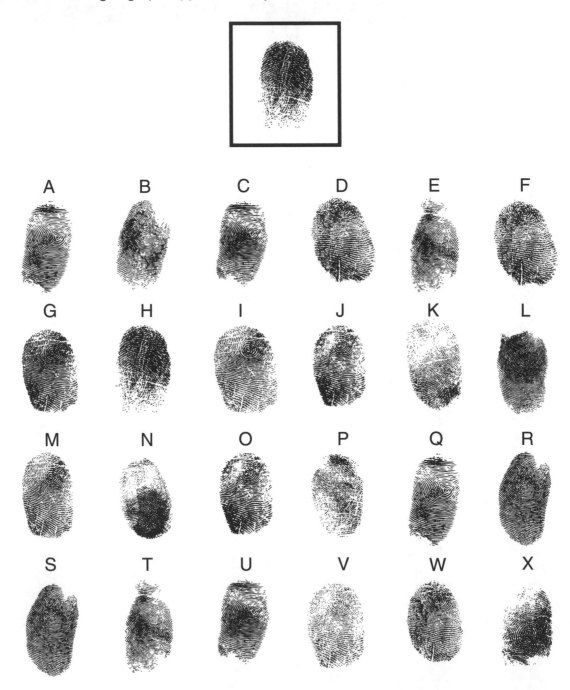

Answers on page 182.

WHAT CHANGED? (PART I)

The consulting detective was at a house party. What did she see in the kitchen? Examine the objects, then turn the page.

WHAT CHANGED? (PART II)

Someone was found unconscious at the house party! They said they'd spotted an intruder and then everything went dark. The consulting detective immediately spotted that one object changed position, and that object was found to be the hastily cleaned weapon. From memory, can you work out what changed position?

Answers on page 182.

WHAT THE CONSULTING
DETECTIVE SAW (PART I)

Study this picture of the crime scene for 1 minute, then turn the page.

WHAT THE CONSULTING
DETECTIVE SAW (PART II)

(Do not read this until you have read the previous page!) Which image exactly matches the crime scene?

Answer on page 182.

A "HELLO HER SMOCKS" ANAGRAM

Below is a quotation from a Sherlock Holmes story. Fill in the blanks in each sentence with a word that is an anagram (rearrangement) of the capitalized word(s).

BONUS: Name the Sherlock Holmes adventure from which this quotation is drawn.

"It is one of those cases where the art of the ROE SNARE _____ should be used rather for the FIG SNIT _____ of DILATES _____ than for the acquiring of fresh VEIN CEDE _____. The tragedy has been so uncommon, so complete and of such RENAL OPS _____ importance to so many people, that we are suffering from a PORT HALE _____ of surmise, conjecture, and PITHY SHOES _____. The difficulty is to CHAT ED _____ the framework of fact—of absolute DINE NEBULA _____ fact—from the embellishments of SHIRE TOTS _____ and reporters. Then, having established ourselves upon this sound basis, it is our duty to see what FENCE REINS _____ may be drawn and what are the ACE LIPS _____ points upon which the whole mystery turns."

Answers on page 182.

INTERNATIONAL FUGITIVES

This was a busy week for Interpol, the international law enforcement agency. Five different criminals from the international "10 Most Wanted" list were apprehended, each in a different country and on a different day. None of the five committed the same crime. Using only the clues below, match each captured fugitive to his crime, and determine the date and location (country) in which he was finally apprehended.

1. Cal Calumnet wasn't apprehended in France.

2. The robbery suspect was captured 3 days before Ben Blackforth.

3. Gil Grendle was wanted for either robbery or arson.

4. Of Ben Blackforth and whoever was captured on October 7th, one was wanted for the arson and the other was tracked down in Sweden.

5. The October 5th capture was of either Cal Calumnet or the man wanted for tax evasion.

6. The forger was captured 2 days before the arrest in Uganda.

7. The arrest in France occurred sometime after that of Dale Dornmer.

8. Neither Dale Dornmer nor Cal Calumnet was captured in Peru.

		Criminals					Crimes					Countries				
		Blackforth	Calumnet	Dornmer	Filcher	Grendle	Arson	Blackmail	Forgery	Robbery	Tax evasion	France	Moldova	Peru	Sweden	Uganda
Dates	October 3															
	October 4															
	October 5															
	October 6															
	October 7															
Countries	France															
	Moldova															
	Peru															
	Sweden															
	Uganda															
Crimes	Arson															
	Blackmail															
	Forgery															
	Robbery															
	Tax evasion															

Dates	Criminals	Crimes	Countries
October 3			
October 4			
October 5			
October 6			
October 7			

95

 Answers on page 182.

INTERCEPTION

You've intercepted a message that is meant to reveal a location for an upcoming meeting between two criminal masterminds. The only problem is, the message shows many place names. Can you figure out the right location?

CROATIA

FINLAND

CHILE

GRENADA

GHANA

SAMOA

Answers on page 183.

A STUDY IN SHERLOCK

Early in his acquaintance with Sherlock Holmes, Dr. Watson wrote: "I pondered over our short conversation, however, and endeavoured to draw my deductions from it. He said that he would acquire no knowledge which did not bear upon his object. Therefore all the knowledge which he possessed was such as would be useful to him. I enumerated in my own mind all the various points upon which he had shown me that he was exceptionally well-informed. I even took a pencil and jotted them down. I could not help smiling at the document when I had completed it."

Can you match each category with Watson's descriptions of Holmes' knowledge in that category? Some descriptions are used for more than one category.

Accurate, but unsystematic

Feeble

Immense

Nil

Practical, but limited

Profound

Variable

1. Literature _____

2. Philosophy _____

3. Astronomy _____

4. Politics _____

5. Botany _____

6. Geology _____

7. Chemistry _____

8. Anatomy _____

9. Sensational Literature _____

Answers on page 183.

ANNA'S ALIBIS

Anna is in a real pickle. The police are convinced she was involved in a break-in last week, even though she swears she was nowhere near the scene of the crime when it took place! Help her sort out her defense by matching each of her corroborating alibis for the night in question with their correct time and location, and determining the relationship with each (friend, cousin, etc.).

1. Anna's Ewing Avenue alibi was either her co-worker or the person who was with her at 10:00pm.

2. Penny Pugh isn't Anna's cousin.

3. Lina Lopez was with Anna sometime after she was on Delancey Road, and thirty minutes before Anna was with her co-worker.

4. Of Anna's 8:00pm and 10:00pm alibis, one was her neighbor and the other was with her on Border Lane.

5. Norma Neet was with Anna one hour after she was on Delancey Road.

6. Penny Pugh, the bartender, and Anna's two alibis on First Street and Ewing Avenue were four different people.

7. Anna's friend was with her on First Street that night, but not at 9:30pm.

8. Anna spent some time with her bartender (who isn't Oda Osborn) that night at her favorite bar on Capitol Street.

		Alibis					Relations					Locations				
		Lina Lopez	Maddy Meyer	Norma Neet	Oda Osborn	Penny Pugh	Bartender	Cousin	Co-worker	Friend	Neighbor	Border Ln.	Capitol St.	Delancey Rd.	Ewing Ave.	First St.
Times	8:00pm															
	8:30pm															
	9:00pm															
	9:30pm															
	10:00pm															
Locations	Border Ln.															
	Capitol St.															
	Delancey Rd.															
	Ewing Ave.															
	First St.															
Relations	Bartender															
	Cousin															
	Co-worker															
	Friend															
	Neighbor															

Times	Alibis	Relations	Locations
8:00pm			
8:30pm			
9:00pm			
9:30pm			
10:00pm			

99

Answers on page 183.

THE ADVENTURE OF THE
NORWOOD BUILDER

Each word or phrase in all capitals in the Sherlock Holmes quotation below is contained within the group of letters. Words can be found horizontally, vertically, or diagonally. They may read either forward or backward.

"From the point of view of the criminal EXPERT," said Mr. Sherlock Holmes, "London has become a singularly UNINTERESTING city since the death of the late LAMENTED Professor Moriarty."

"I can hardly think that you would find many DECENT citizens to agree with you," I answered.

"Well, well, I must not be SELFISH," said he, with a smile, as he pushed back his chair from the breakfast-table. "The COMMUNITY is certainly the gainer, and no one the loser, save the poor out-of-work SPECIALIST, whose OCCU-PATION has gone. With that man in the field, one's morning paper presented INFINITE possibilities. Often it was only the smallest trace, Watson, the faintest indication, and yet it was enough to tell me that the great MALIGNANT brain was there, as the gentlest TREMORS of the edges of the web remind one of the foul spider which lurks in the centre. PETTY thefts, WANTON assaults, purposeless outrage—to the man who held the CLUE all could be worked into one connected whole. To the SCIENTIFIC student of the higher criminal world, no capital in Europe offered the ADVANTAGES which LONDON then pos-sessed. But now— —" He shrugged his shoulders in humorous DEPRECATION of the state of things which he had himself done so much to produce.

```
N T T R E M O R S N F Y G V Y
O S H E U Y V Y O Z X V H M T
I I M S L L E D P E T T Y U I
T L U C C N N F V Z Q X L N N
A A S I G O H S I F L E S I U
C I M E L I H A D N X B V N M
E C A N G T B N B A F K A T M
R E L T I A F O G K C J I E O
P P I I N P T T N E C E D R C
E S G F F U A N R Y X G W E U
D C N I I C K A A R C D L S Q
I W A C N C C W S V O Y Z T C
H W N M I O Q O K V D H K I D
M L T I T D E T N E M A L N R
K Y Z J E P J T R E P X E G T
```

A "HOCK MESHES ROLL" ANAGRAM

Below is a quotation from a Sherlock Holmes story. Fill in the blanks in each sentence with a word that is an anagram (rearrangement) of the capitalized word(s).

BONUS: Name the Sherlock Holmes adventure from which this quotation is drawn.

"It is not cold which makes me shiver," said the woman in a low voice, changing her seat as DEER QUEST _____ .

"What, then?"

"It is fear, Mr. Holmes. It is ERR ROT _____." She raised her veil as she spoke, and we could see that she was indeed in a ALIBI PET _____ state of GIANT IOTA _____, her face all drawn and grey, with restless THEN FRIDGE _____ eyes, like those of some hunted animal. Her SAFE TRUE _____ and figure were those of a woman of thirty, but her hair was shot with TAMPER RUE _____ grey, and her expression was weary and GAG HARD _____. Sherlock Holmes ran her over with one of his quick, all-comprehensive glances.

"You must not fear," said he NIGHTY SOLO _____, bending forward and patting her FARM ROE _____. "We shall soon set matters right, I have no BUD TO _____. You have come in by RAN IT _____ this morning, I see."

Answers on page 183.

WHAT WENT MISSING? (PART I)

The consulting detective visited a client's rooms one day. What did he see? Examine the objects, then turn the page.

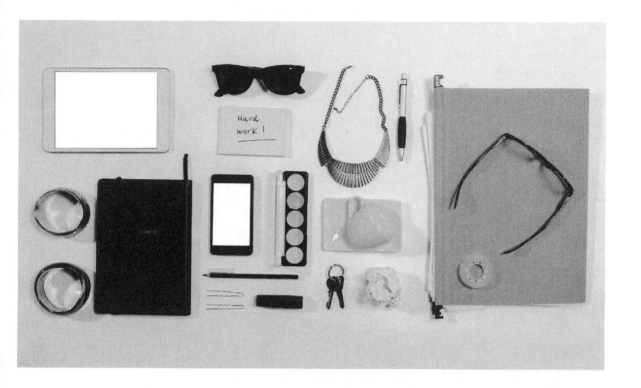

WHAT WENT MISSING? (PART II)

The next day, the client went missing. Called in to help, the consulting detective saw that something else went missing as well. From memory, can you work out what went missing?

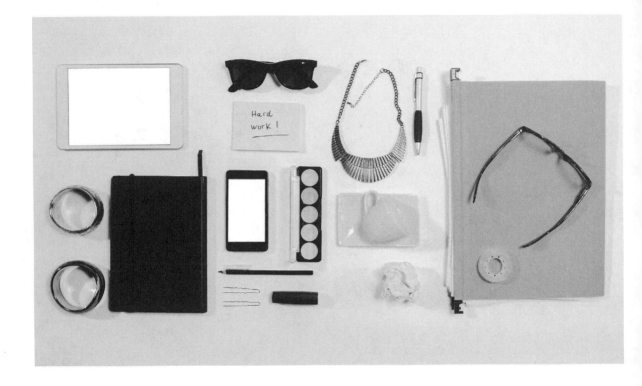

Answer on page 183.

A SAD STATISTIC

Cryptograms are messages in substitution code. Break the code to read the message. For example, THE SMART CAT might become FVO QWGDF JGF if **F** is substituted for **T, V** for **H, O** for **E,** and so on.

RDA MAOZAJRKCA LB QRLHAJ KOR RDKR EQ OAZL-TAOAP EQ JLR TAOX DECD. LJHX BETA RL RAJ MAO-ZAJR IECDR WA OAZLTAOAP.

A MYSTERIOUS EVENT

Cryptograms are messages in substitution code. Break the code to read the message. For example, THE SMART CAT might become FVO QWGDF JGF if **F** is substituted for **T, V** for **H, O** for **E,** and so on.

SCI YITO 1911 DKVLGVIJ T KLSTPGI RTQI LA TOS SCIAS—SCI HLKT GDQT WTQ QSLGIK AOLH SCI GLUVOI PY TK IHMGLYII. CI WTQ RTUBCS SWL YITOQ GTSIO TKJ SCI MTDKSDKB WTQ OISUOKIJ SL DSQ CLHI.

Answers on page 184.

MARKED BILLS

The local police have been tracking a series of marked bills that were stolen during a recent string of bank robberies, in an effort to capture the perpetrators. So far, five such bills have been located. Each was used in a different place and on a different day, and each bill was of a different denomination (such as a $10 or a $20). Using only the clues below, match each marked bill to the date and location in which it was spent, and determine the serial number and denomination of each one.

1. C-918303 was used 8 days after the bill that popped up in Midvale.

2. The $100 bill wasn't spent on April 13th.

3. P-101445 was either the $20 bill or the one used on April 5.

4. The $5 bill with the serial number B-492841 was used 4 days after F-667280, but not in Finsberg.

5. The Midvale bill was used 4 days after G-718428 was passed somewhere in Torbin.

6. The marked $20 bill was spent 4 days after the one in Nettleton.

7. Neither the $10 bill nor the $100 bill was used on April 1st.

		Serials					Locations					Denominations				
		B-492841	C-918303	F-667280	G-718428	P-101445	Finsberg	Midvale	Nettleton	Torbin	Uteville	$5	$10	$20	$50	$100
Dates	April 1															
	April 5															
	April 9															
	April 13															
	April 17															
Denominations	$5										
	$10										
	$20										
	$50										
	$100										
Locations	Finsberg					
	Midvale					
	Nettleton					
	Torbin					
	Uteville					

Dates	Serials	Locations	Denominations
April 1			
April 5			
April 9			
April 13			
April 17			

Answers on page 184.

BANK ROBBERIES

Bledsoe County has been beset by a gang of bank robbers! Five different banks, each in a different town, have been robbed by the same gang in just the past 10 days. The total amount stolen from each bank was never the same, and the gang never robbed more than one bank on any given day. Using only the clues below, help track down the gang by matching each bank to the town it is in, and determine the date each was robbed as well as how much was stolen.

1. The most expensive robbery happened 2 days after Bell Largo was hit.

2. The gang got away with $4,800 2 days before they robbed another bank of $2,500.

3. Of Apex Bank and Wellspring, one was robbed on June 11th and the other lost $4,800.

4. The bank in Grumley was either Wellspring or the one robbed on June 9th.

5. Bell Largo was robbed 2 days before the bank in Cold Spring.

6. The $1,000 robbery took place 2 days before Moneycorp was hit, but not in Yountville.

7. The gang robbed a bank (which wasn't Apex) in Tahoe on June 7th.

8. Cold Spring's bank was robbed on June 11th.

		Banks					Towns					Amounts				
		Apex	Bell Largo	First Trust	Moneycorp	Wellspring	Cold Spring	Grumley	Longwood	Tahoe	Yountville	$1,000	$1,600	$2,500	$4,800	$10,200
Dates	June 3															
	June 5															
	June 7															
	June 9															
	June 11															
Amounts	$1,000															
	$1,600															
	$2,500															
	$4,800															
	$10,200															
Towns	Cold Spring															
	Grumley															
	Longwood															
	Tahoe															
	Yountville															

Dates	Banks	Towns	Amounts
June 3			
June 5			
June 7			
June 9			
June 11			

Answers on page 184.

THE ADVENTURE OF BLACK PETER

Each word or phrase in all capitals in the Sherlock Holmes quotation below is contained within the group of letters. Words can be found horizontally, vertically, or diagonally. They may read either forward or backward.

I have never known my friend to be in BETTER form, both mental and physical, than in the year '95. His increasing FAME had brought with it an IMMENSE practice, and I should be guilty of an INDISCRETION if I were even to hint at the identity of some of the ILLUSTRIOUS clients who crossed our humble THRESHOLD in Baker Street. Holmes, however, like all great ARTISTS, lived for his art's sake, and, save in the case of the Duke of Holdernesse, I have seldom known him claim any large REWARD for his INESTIMABLE services. So UNWORLDLY was he—or so CAPRICIOUS—that he frequently REFUSED his help to the powerful and WEALTHY where the problem made no APPEAL to his sympathies, while he would devote weeks of most INTENSE application to the AFFAIRS of some humble client whose case presented those strange and DRAMATIC qualities which appealed to his imagination and CHALLENGED his INGENUITY.

```
W S O Y D R A M A T I C Y K N
K C U Y T I U N E G N I A V O
N D N O W A D U M B V N F Y I
V U B S I C P E Q P W T F H T
D N G Q U C U P S K Q E A T E
E W R A A O I J E U Q N I L R
G O E A R M I R R A F S R A C
N R T R T K E R P O L E S E S
E L T E I E M R T A M Y R W I
L D E W S S A Z S S C S I R D
L L B A T N F O J M U S L I N
A Y U R S E L S Z J L L S L I
H T J D D M Z M I K S Y L U P
C E L B A M I T S E N I N I V
Y N B D H I T H R E S H O L D
```

Answers on page 184.

Cryptograms are messages in substitution code. Break the code to read the message. For example, THE SMART CAT might become FVO QWGDF JGF if **F** is substituted for **T, V** for **H, O** for **E,** and so on.

BONUS: Who is the speaker? Which story is the source of the quote?

"OXPLP CLP OTH KQPNOZHGN TCZOZGV SHL QN CO OXP HQONPO. OXP HGP ZN TXPOXPL CGW ILZEP XCN FPPG IHEEZOOPM CO CDD; OXP NPIHGM ZN, TXCO ZN OXP ILZEP CGM XHT TCN ZO IHEEZOOPM? HS IHQLNP, ZS ML. EHLOZEPL'N NQLEZNP NXHQDM FP IHLLPIO, CGM TP CLP MPCDZGV TZOX SHLIPN HQONZMP OXP HLMZGCLW DCTN HS GCOQLP, OXPLP ZN CG PGM HS HQL ZGRPNOZVCOZHG. FQO TP CLP FHQGM OH PUXCQNO CDD HOXPL XWJHOXPNPN FPSHLP SCDDZGV FCIB QJHG OXZN HGP. Z OXZGB TP'DD NXQO OXCO TZGMHT CVCZG, ZS WHQ MHG'O EZGM. ZO ZN C NZGVQDCL OXZGV, FQO Z SZGM OXCO C IHGIPGOLCOPM COEHNJXPLP XPDJN C IHGIPGOLCOZHG HS OXHQVXO. Z XCRP GHO JQNXPM ZO OH OXP DPGVOX HS VPOOZGV ZGOH C FHU OH OXZGB, FQO OXCO ZN OXP DHVZICD HQOIHEP HS EW IHGRZIOZHGN."

Answers on page 184.

WHAT WENT MISSING? (PART I)

The consulting detective visited the dressing room of the actress who had received threats. Examine the objects, then turn the page.

WHAT WENT MISSING? (PART II)

Overnight, the actress got sick from poison and was rushed to the hospital! The consulting detective noted something missing from her dressing room and suspected it contained the poison. From memory, can you work out what went missing?

Answer on page 185.

INTERCEPTION

You've intercepted a message that is meant to reveal a location for an upcoming meeting between two criminal masterminds. The only problem is, the message doesn't make sense. Can you figure out the right location?

WAUKESHA

SOUTH

ISLINGTON

GAULT

OMAN

DORIC

Answer on page 185.

RARE WINES

Georgina Guernsey's prized wine cellar was broken into last night, and five of her most rare bottles were stolen! She's absolutely beside herself... especially since she was planning on having her annual Spring garden party this weekend. Help the police figure out what's missing by matching each missing bottle of wine to its type, vintage year, and country of origin.

1. The Friambliss was bottled 8 years before the French wine.

2. The syrah, the Friambliss, and the Spanish wine were bottled in three different years.

3. The Weimerund isn't a merlot, and it wasn't bottled in 1958.

4. Of the Ece Suss and the 1970 bottle, one is from Greece and the other is a merlot.

5. The 1958 bottle is either the pinot gris or the Spanish wine.

6. Ania Branco wasn't ever made in France.

7. The Italian wine was bottled 4 years before the Spanish one, which wasn't the chardonnay.

8. Of the merlot and the pinot gris, one was from France and the other was a 1962 vintage.

9. The 1966 wine wasn't a syrah.

		Wines					Types					Countries			
		Ania Branco	Ece Suss	Friambliss	Vendemmia	Weimerund	Chardonnay	Merlot	Pinot Gris	Pinot Noir	Syrah	France	Greece	Italy	Portugal	Spain
Vintages	1954															
	1958															
	1962															
	1966															
	1970															
Countries	France															
	Greece															
	Italy															
	Portugal															
	Spain															
Types	Chardonnay															
	Merlot															
	Pinot Gris															
	Pinot Noir															
	Syrah															

Vintages	Wines	Types	Countries
1954			
1958			
1962			
1966			
1970			

Answers on page 185.

DESCRIBING SHERLOCK HOLMES

Cryptograms are messages in substitution code. Break the code to read the message. For example, THE SMART CAT might become FVO QWGDF JGF if **F** is substituted for **T**, **V** for **H, O** for **E,** and so on.

BONUS: Who is the speaker of this quote? Which story is the source of the quote?

"JM JK ACM RZKW MC RUEIRKK MLR JARUEIRK-KJXDR," LR ZAKSRIRT SJML Z DZONL. "LCDBRK JK Z DJMMDR MCC KVJRAMJPJV PCI BW MZKMRK— JM ZEEICZVLRK MC VCDT-XDCCTRTARKK. J VCODT JBZNJAR LJK NJQJAN Z PIJRAT Z DJMMDR EJAVL CP MLR DZMRKM QRNRMZXDR ZDFZDCJT, ACM COM CP BZDRQCDRAVR, WCO OATRIKMZAT, XOM KJBEDW COM CP Z KEJIJM CP JAGOJIW JA CITRI MC LZQR ZA ZVVOIZMR JTRZ CP MLR RPPRVMK. MC TC LJB HOK- MJVR, J MLJAF MLZM LR SCODT MZFR JM LJBKRDP SJML MLR KZBR IRZTJARKK. LR ZEERZIK MC LZQR Z EZKKJCA PCI TRPJAJMR ZAT RUZVM FACSDRTNR."

WHAT THE CONSULTING
DETECTIVE SAW (PART I)

Study this picture of the crime scene for 1 minute, then turn the page.

WHAT THE CONSULTING
DETECTIVE SAW (PART II)

(Do not read this until you have read the previous page!) Which image exactly matches the crime scene?

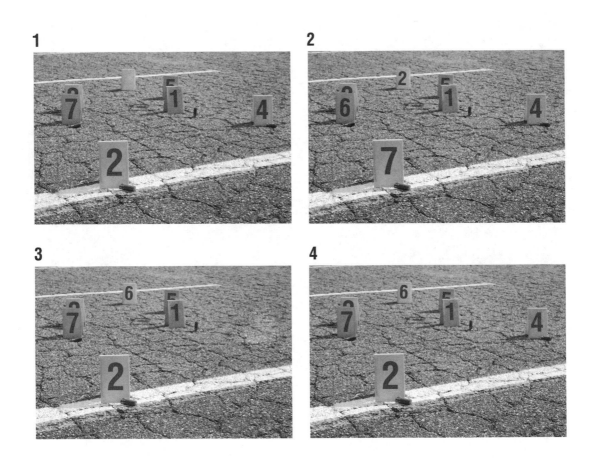

Answer on page 185.

FINGERPRINT MATCH

There are 12 sets of fingerprints. Find each match.

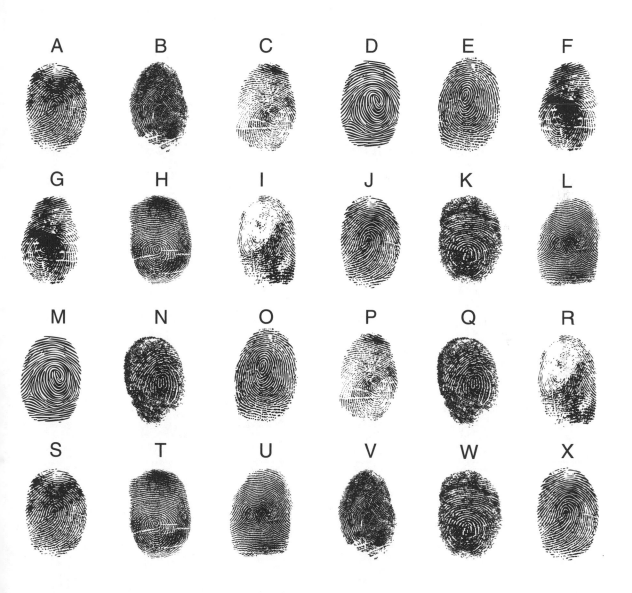

Answers on page 185.

THE ADVENTURE OF THE
GOLDEN PINCE-NEZ

Each word or phrase in all capitals in the Sherlock Holmes quotation below is contained within the group of letters. Words can be found horizontally, vertically, or diagonally. They may read either forward or backward.

It was a wild, TEMPESTUOUS night, towards the close of NOVEMBER. Holmes and I sat together in silence all the EVENING, he engaged with a powerful lens DECIPHERING the remains of the original INSCRIPTION upon a PALIMPSEST, I deep in a recent TREATISE upon SURGERY. Outside the wind HOWLED down Baker Street, while the rain beat FIERCELY against the windows. It was strange there, in the very depths of the town, with ten miles of man's HANDIWORK on every side of us, to feel the iron grip of NATURE, and to be conscious that to the huge ELEMENTAL forces all London was no more than the molehills that dot the fields. I walked to the window, and looked out on the DESERTED street. The occasional lamps gleamed on the expanse of MUDDY road and shining pavement. A single CAB was SPLASHING its way from the OXFORD STREET end.

```
U T E M P E S T U O U S J G E
G G M Q B T J N T H X E U N S
G N I R E H P I C E D D L I I
P I G D E S E R T E D A O N T
A H Q Z B H L S D E T X N E A
L S U K G P U E R N F O R V E
I A X G V R L U E O I E C E R
M L Q F G W T M R T B B Q O T
P P Z E O A E D P M X P A Z U
S S R H N L S I E L B R E C D
E Y S W E T R V G K E P M R E
S Z B R R C O F I E R C E L Y
T U R E S N W B W I M U D D Y
X A E N S S K R O W I D N A H
C T I X S V Q M H B S P S D F
```

Answers on page 186.

SMUGGLED ELECTRONICS

The F.B.I. has received a tip-off that a notorious criminal gang is planning to smuggle counterfeit electronics out of Amity Airport this morning. The informant indicated that 5 different shipments (each containing a different type of consumer electronic device) would go out, each on a different flight. Help the agents bust this smuggling ring by matching each illegal shipment to its flight number, departure time, and gate number.

1. The cell phones are going out of either gate 6 or gate 11.

2. The flight at gate 18 will leave 7 minutes before the one out of gate 3.

3. The earliest departure isn't at gate 7.

4. Flight 92 is either the one with the laptops or the one leaving at 8:17am.

5. Flight 233 will depart sometime after 8:05am.

6. The plane that departs at 8:24am, the one with the counterfeit tablets, and the one leaving from gate 11 are three different flights.

7. Of the tablet and the laptop shipments, one will leave at 8:31am and the other is stored on flight 356.

8. Of the plane at gate 3 and Flight 233, one has a shipment of flat-screen televisions and the other will depart at 8:17am.

9. The watch shipment is scheduled to depart sometime before the plane with the illegal cell phones (which isn't flight 108)

10. Flight 356 will leave 7 minutes after the plane at gate 18.

	Flights					Gates					Items				
	92	108	233	356	510	3	6	7	11	18	Cell phones	Laptops	Tablets	Televisions	Watches
Departures 8:03am															
8:10am															
8:17am															
8:24am															
8:31am															
Items Cell phones															
Laptops															
Tablets															
Televisions															
Watches															
Gates 3															
6															
7															
11															
18															

Departures	Flights	Gates	Items
8:03am			
8:10am			
8:17am			
8:24am			
8:31am			

125

Answers on page 186.

A "CORK SHELL HOMES" ANAGRAM

Below is a quotation from a Sherlock Holmes story. Fill in the blanks in each sentence with a word that is an anagram (rearrangement) of the capitalized word(s).

BONUS: Name the Sherlock Holmes adventure from which this quotation is drawn.

Sherlock Holmes was a man who seldom took RICE EXES _____ for EXEC'S RISE _____ sake. Few men were capable of greater CUR MAULS _____ effort, and he was DOUBLY TUNED _____ one of the finest boxers of his TWIG HE _____ that I have ever seen; but he looked upon aimless bodily TIRE OXEN _____ as a waste of energy, and he seldom REST BRIDE _____ himself save when there was some professional object to be served. Then he was absolutely UNIT GRIN _____ and FAILING DEBATE _____. That he should have kept himself in TIN GRAIN _____ under such SCARCEST CUMIN _____ is remarkable, but his diet was usually of the REPASTS _____, and his habits were simple to the verge of TEARY SUIT _____.

Answers on page 186.

WHAT CHANGED? (PART I)

The consulting detective's friends like to challenge him. They lined up the series of bottles seen below. Examine the objets, then turn the page.

WHAT CHANGED? (PART II)

The detective's friends made one change to the objects and showed them to him again. From memory, can you say what changed?

Answer on page 186.

FILL IN THE EMPTY HOUSE

Complete each quote from the Sherlock Holmes story "The Empty House" with one of the choices.

1. A minute examination of the circumstances served only to make the case more _____.

    A. bizarre

    B. complex

    C. obvious

2. With a snarl of contempt he turned upon his heel, and I saw his curved back and white _____ disappear among the throng.

    A. side-whiskers

    B. beard

    C. head

3. "Well, then, about that _____. I had no serious difficulty in getting out of it, for the very simple reason that I never was in it."

    A. chasm

    B. bog

    C. abyss

4. "_____ is the best antidote to sorrow, my dear Watson," said he; "and I have a piece of work for us both to-night which, if we can bring it to a successful conclusion, will in itself justify a man's life on this planet."

    A. labor

    B. success

    C. work

5. "Am I such a(n) _____, Watson, that I should erect an obvious dummy, and expect that some of the sharpest men in Europe would be deceived by it?"

    A. silly fool

    B. farcical bungler

    C. obvious idiot

          Answers on page 186.

FOR STAGE AND SCREEN

Every name listed below belongs to an actor who played Holmes in a Sherlock Holmes adaptation. Names can be found in a straight line horizontally, vertically, or diagonally. They may be read either forward or backward.

ALAN WHEATLEY

ARTHUR WONTNER

BASIL RATHBONE

BENEDICT CUMBERBATCH

CHARLTON HESTON

CHRISTOPHER LEE

CLIVE BROOK

EILLE NORWOOD

GEOFFREY WHITEHEAD

HARRY ARTHUR SAINTSBURY

IAN MCKELLEN

JEREMY BRETT

JOHN BARRYMORE

JONNY LEE MILLER

LEONARD NIMOY

MACK SENNETT

MAURICE COSTELLO

MICHAEL CAINE

NICHOLAS ROWE

NICOL WILLIAMSON

PATRICK MACNEE

ROBERT DOWNEY, JR.

ROBERT STEPHENS

WILLIAM GILLETTE

```
B E N E D I C T C U M B E R B A T C H Y H
H A R R Y A R T H U R S A I N T S B U R Y
E W O R S A L O H C I N C U Y I N A R K Y
O N C I M N C N P P T A E Q F M T U M R O
T L U S N E H P E T S T R E B O R B N Y K
E N I A C L E A H C I M T L V O M W Y R Y
C H A R L T O N H E S T O N M Q G P A W Y
D A E H E T I H W Y E R F F O E G B P S J
Y L R E D I D L B S V I E Y H W L A A A W
E A N I C O L W I L L I A M S O N S T R M
L N E T T E L L I G M A I L L I W I R T A
T R E L L I M E E L Y N N O J A X L I H C
A Y O M I N D R A N O E L X Z I O R C U K
E A Y R O B E R T D O W N E Y J R A K R S
H K O O R B E V I L C R J Q M X X T M W E
W N E L L E K C M N A I W N D R W H A O N
N J E R E M Y B R E T T N O W N J B C N N
A J O H N B A R R Y M O R E O G P O N T E
L C H R I S T O P H E R L E E D A N E N T
A Q Y W W Z X Q T Q F F W F B Y X E E E T
Q M A U R I C E C O S T E L L O A V V R K
```

131

Answers on page 187.

A "MS HOLLER CHOKES" ANAGRAM

Below is a quotation from a Sherlock Holmes story. Fill in the blanks in each sentence with a word that is an anagram (rearrangement) of the capitalized word(s).

BONUS: Name the Sherlock Holmes adventure from which this quotation is drawn.

"Porlock, Watson, is a POMMEL DUNE _____, a mere identification mark; but behind it lies a shifty and VISA EVE _____ personality. In a former letter he RANK FLY _____ informed me that the name was not his own, and FEE DID _____ me ever to trace him among the MEETING _____ millions of this great city. Porlock is important, not for HE FILMS _____, but for the great man with whom he is in touch. PUT RICE _____ to yourself the pilot fish with the HARKS _____, the jackal with the lion—anything that is insignificant in companionship with what is BAILED FROM _____: not only FEDORA LIMB _____, Watson, but ITS SIREN _____—in the highest degree SIRE SNIT _____. That is where he comes within my purview. You have heard me speak of FOR SPORES _____ ARMY TRIO _____?"

Answers on page 187.

WHAT THE CONSULTING DETECTIVE SAW (PART I)

Study this picture of the crime scene for 1 minute, then turn the page.

WHAT THE CONSULTING
DETECTIVE SAW (PART II)

(Do not read this until you have read the previous page!) Which image exactly matches the crime scene?

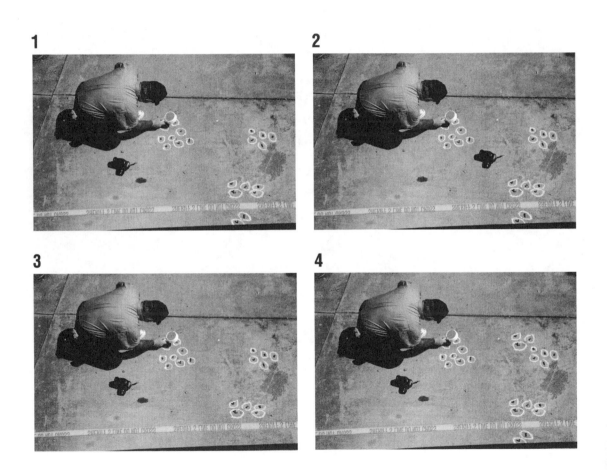

1

2

3

4

Answer on page 187.

WHAT WENT MISSING? (PART I)

The consulting detective met his client on Thursday about a set of thefts. The detective toured the house, including the kitchen. Examine the room, then turn the page.

WHAT WENT MISSING? (PART II)

Overnight, more things were stolen. The consulting detective returned to the house and figured out immediately what had gone missing. From memory, can you work out what went missing?

Answers on page 187.

A "SHH COOKER SMELL" ANAGRAM

Below is a quotation from a Sherlock Holmes story. Fill in the blanks in each sentence with a word that is an anagram (rearrangement) of the capitalized word(s).

BONUS: Name the Sherlock Holmes adventure from which this quotation is drawn.

It was difficult to FREE US _____ any of Sherlock Holmes' requests, for they were always so exceedingly FINE DIET _____, and put forward with such a quiet air of SEAM TRY _____. I felt, however, that when Whitney was once CONNED IF _____ in the cab my mission was practically CHEMICAL PODS _____; and for the rest, I could not wish anything better than to be AIDES ASCOT _____ with my friend in one of those singular EVADER NUTS _____ which were the normal condition of his SCENE EXIT. In a few minutes I had written my note, paid Whitney's bill, led him out to the cab, and seen him driven through the ARK SENDS _____. In a very short time a CIDER PET _____ figure had emerged from the MOUND PIE _____ _____ (2 words), and I was walking down the street with Sherlock Holmes. For two streets he LED HUFFS _____ along with a bent back and an ANTIC RUNE _____ foot. Then, glancing quickly round, he straightened himself out and burst into a EARTHY _____ fit of laughter.

Answers on page 188.

STOLEN STREET SIGNS

Someone's been stealing street signs in Starrington! Every week (always on a Saturday night) a new sign has gone missing. Each time it's a different type of sign (stop sign, yield sign, etc.) in a different part of town. Help the police track down the thief by matching each sign to the date it went missing and its original location at the intersection of two streets.

1. Of the speed limit sign and the one that was at Barnacle Road, one went missing on July 25th and the other was at the corner of Tarragon Lane.

2. Quinella Street doesn't intersect with Falstaff St.

3. The speed limit sign was stolen sometime after the one from Ralston Avenue.

4. The Amble Lane sign didn't go missing on August 1st.

5. The Dwight Street sign went missing one week before the one from Tarragon Lane.

6. The one-way sign was stolen 1 week before the Casper Boulevard sign, and 3 weeks before the one on Selby Street.

7. The dead end sign, the stop sign, the one from Selby Street, and the two stolen before July 14th were five different signs.

8. One of the missing signs stood at the corner of Selby Street and Barnacle Road. Selby Street doesn't have any "No Parking" signs.

9. Peabody Lane, which has no "Dead End" signs anywhere near it, intersects with either Dwight Street or Everett Avenue (but not both).

10. The stop sign went missing sometime before the sign at Peabody Lane (but not on July 18th).

	Signs						Streets						Streets					
	Dead End	No Parking	One Way	Speed Limit	Stop	Yield	Amble Ln.	Barnacle Rd.	Casper Blvd.	Dwight St.	Everett Ave.	Falstaff St.	Oracle Rd.	Peabody Ln.	Quinella St.	Ralston Ave.	Selby St.	Tarragon Ln.
July 4th																		
July 11th																		
July 18th																		
July 25th																		
August 1st																		
August 8th																		
Oracle Rd.																		
Peabody Ln.																		
Quinella St.																		
Ralston Ave.																		
Selby St.																		
Tarragon Ln.																		
Amble Ln.																		
Barnacle Rd.																		
Casper Blvd.																		
Dwight St.																		
Everett Ave.																		
Falstaff St.																		

Dates	Signs	Streets	Streets
July 4th			
July 11th			
July 18th			
July 25th			
August 1st			
August 8th			

Answers on page 188.

THE REIGATE PUZZLE

Each word or phrase in all capitals in the Sherlock Holmes quotation below is contained within the group of letters. Words can be found horizontally, vertically, or diagonally. They may read either forward or backward.

On referring to my notes I see that it was upon the 14th of April that I received a TELEGRAM from Lyons which informed me that Holmes was LYING ILL in the Hotel Dulong. Within twenty-four hours I was in his SICK-ROOM, and was relieved to find that there was nothing formidable in his SYMPTOMS. Even his iron CONSTITUTION, however, had broken down under the STRAIN of an investigation which had extended over two months, during which period he had never worked less than fifteen hours a day, and had more than once, as he assured me, kept to his TASK for five days at a stretch. Even the TRIUM-PHANT issue of his labors could not save him from REACTION after so terrible an EXERTION, and at a time when Europe was ringing with his name and when his room was literally ankle-deep with CONGRATULATORY telegrams I found him a prey to the blackest DEPRESSION. Even the knowledge that he had succeeded where the police of three countries had failed, and that he had OUTMANOEUVRED at every point the most accomplished SWINDLER in Europe, was insufficient to ROUSE him from his nervous PROSTRATION.

```
N W E D N Y X T E T K A A I Q C W O R
O V K E O N F G V Y Y F O T E K Q L R
I Q D R I R C D I Y K I N S Q E G S W
T E Q V S L C V Q Z Q A W O H T E Y L
U C X U S Z L K Q H H I D S C G D M Y
T V R E E Y P B O P N N E Q Y O X P I
I Z M O R B A H M D V O V R P W F T N
T Q P N P T R U L D S I O N E S L O G
S J L A E T I E U L D T Z T I M B M I
N G A M D R R O M W A A X L B A L S L
O I B T T E X K N L Z R E A N R R H L
C O Z U R K Q T U S H T F M V G S T Q
R I W O Z E I T Y W E S Q H B E I N S
K A U F T O A F G K M O V E W L C D I
S S D J W R I C Z D Y R H P U E K M H
E Y P F G K F W T D R P W K G T R L Z
O G G N G S M B F I D F T A S K O X N
J L O K I S V U S T O V V W E W O S Q
G C S C J K J E E E K N D S M N M X C
```

Answers on page 188.

FAMOUS FIRST LINES

How well do you know the Holmes canon? Match the first line of each story to the story's title.

1. On glancing over my notes of the seventy odd cases in which I have during the last eight years studied the methods of my friend Sherlock Holmes, I find many tragic, some comic, a large number merely strange, but none commonplace; for, working as he did rather for the love of his art than for the acquirement of wealth, he refused to associate himself with any investigation which did not tend towards the unusual, and even the fantastic.

2. We were seated at breakfast one morning, my wife and I, when the maid brought in a telegram.

3. It is years since the incidents of which I speak took place, and yet it is with diffidence that I allude to them.

4. I had called upon my friend Sherlock Holmes upon the second morning after Christmas, with the intention of wishing him the compliments of the season.

5. An anomaly which often struck me in the character of my friend Sherlock Holmes was that, although in his methods of thought he was the neatest and most methodical of mankind, and although also he affected a certain quiet primness of dress, he was none the less in his personal habits one of the most untidy men that ever drove a fellow lodger to distraction.

A. The Adventure of the Blue Carbuncle

B. The Adventure of the Musgrave Ritual

C. The Boscombe Valley Mystery

D. The Adventure of Charles Augustus Milverton

E. The Adventure of the Speckled Band

Answers on page 188.

WHAT WENT MISSING? (PART I)

The consulting detective met with a nature photographer and writer who had received strange threatening messages. Examine the objects on the writer's desk, then turn the page.

WHAT WENT MISSING? (PART II)

The next day, the writer was hit over the head and rushed to the hospital. The consulting detective went to the scene and immediately spotted that something had been stolen. From memory, can you work out what went missing?

Answer on page 188.

STOP, THIEF!

Cryptograms are messages in substitution code. Break the code to read the message. For example, THE SMART CAT might become FVO QWGDF JGF if **F** is substituted for **T,** **V** for **H, O** for **E,** and so on.

CPC WYH MVYL FGKF FGR QKTYHB CRFRNFPJR UYBF GPB QPEBF NKBR? GPB QPEBF NKBR YV QPUT, FGKF PB. PV 1900, K BGYEF BPURVF QPUT NKUURC, "BGREUYNM GYUTRB AKQQURC," LKB NERKFRC. PV FGR QPUT, KV PVFEHCRE ERDRKFRCUW NYTRB PVFY QEKTR KVC BFRKUB QEYT FGR BURHFG. KB DEYTPBRC PV FGR FPFUR, FGR AHEZUKE ZRFB KLKW HVBNKFGRC. YQ NYHEBR, FGR QPUT YVUW EHVB FGPEFW BRNYVCB, BY DREGKDB OHBFPNR LYHUC GKJR DERJKPURC PQ FGR QPUTBFEPD GKC NYVF-PVHRC.

Answers on page 188.

You've intercepted a message between two criminals. At first glance it doesn't seem to make sense, but can you decipher the true message to reveal the date and location of a meeting?

PET ASP PUT POT AHA SET OFT PAD ESP

ICE FED ODE

ATE USE ORE TIN AFT

AMP APE MEN INT YON

Answers on page 189.

WHAT CHANGED? (PART I)

The consulting detective was at a house party. What did he see on the kitchen table? Examine the objects, then turn the page.

WHAT CHANGED? (PART II)

There was a murder at the house party! The consulting detective immediately spotted that one object changed position, and that object was found to be the hastily cleaned murder weapon. From memory, can you work out what changed position?

Answer on page 189.

A "CHROME ELK SLOSH" ANAGRAM

Below is a quotation from a Sherlock Holmes story. Fill in the blanks in each sentence with a word that is an anagram (rearrangement) of the capitalized word(s).

BONUS: Name the Sherlock Holmes adventure from which this quotation is drawn.

To Sherlock Holmes she is always THE woman. I have seldom heard him OMEN TIN _____ her under any other name. In his eyes she EELS PICS _____ and predominates the whole of her sex. It was not that he felt any MIEN TOO _____ akin to love for Irene Adler. All MOTE IONS _____, and that one particularly, were BARREN HOT _____ to his cold, precise but admirably CABAL DEN _____ mind. He was, I take it, the most perfect reasoning and ob-serving AH MINCE _____ that the world has seen, but as a lover he would have placed himself in a false POTION IS _____. He never spoke of the softer SOAP SINS _____, save with a gibe and a sneer. They were DRAMA BILE _____ things for the observer—excellent for drawing the veil from men's TOE VIMS _____ and actions. But for the trained reasoner to admit such UNION STIRS _____ into his own delicate and finely adjusted MANE TEMPTER _____ was to introduce a distracting factor which might throw a doubt upon all his mental results. Grit in a sensitive NUTRIMENTS _____, or a crack in one of his own high-power lenses, would not be more BUSING DIRT _____ than a strong emotion in a nature such as his. And yet there was but one woman to him, and that woman was the late Irene Adler, of dubious and ELOQUENT BIAS _____ memory.

Answers on page 189.

CHARLES AUGUSTUS MILVERTON

Each word or phrase in all capitals in the Sherlock Holmes quotation below is contained within the group of letters. Words can be found horizontally, vertically, or diagonally. They may read either forward or backward.

"Hum! He's about due. Do you feel a CREEPING, shrinking sensation, Watson, when you stand before the SERPENTS in the Zoo, and see the SLITHERY, GLIDING, VENOMOUS creatures, with their DEADLY eyes and WICKED, flattened faces? Well, that's how MILVERTON impresses me. I've had to do with fifty MURDERERS in my career, but the worst of them never gave me the REPULSION which I have for this fellow. And yet I can't get out of doing BUSINESS with him—indeed, he is here at my INVITATION."

"But who is he?"

"I'll tell you, Watson. He is the KING of all the BLACKMAILERS. Heaven help the man, and still more the woman, whose SECRET and REPUTATION come into the POWER of Milverton! With a SMILING face and a HEART of MARBLE, he will SQUEEZE and squeeze until he has DRAINED them dry."

```
H  N  D  V  J  B  S  U  O  M  O  N  E  V  M  Y  T
C  S  M  I  L  I  N  G  Q  N  S  K  Q  R  A  E  U
T  R  S  G  H  J  G  Y  E  A  R  O  M  O  R  F  E
R  U  E  D  L  S  S  Q  U  E  E  Z  E  C  B  K  N
A  R  R  E  L  I  F  Z  G  Z  L  W  E  P  L  S  K
E  Q  P  C  P  M  D  E  T  Z  I  S  Z  D  E  R  F
H  Y  E  B  S  I  E  I  K  P  A  W  I  C  K  E  D
Q  S  N  U  A  P  N  F  N  W  M  N  N  F  R  R  R
E  L  T  K  V  I  G  D  G  K  O  V  P  E  E  E
S  I  S  U  N  B  A  X  Y  J  C  I  I  B  W  D  P
R  T  L  H  P  B  R  G  E  K  A  S  T  U  O  R  U
K  H  P  E  E  M  D  G  I  G  L  L  A  S  P  U  T
I  E  J  O  L  E  F  B  G  L  B  U  T  I  R  M  A
N  R  D  H  A  B  A  H  P  M  W  P  I  N  A  B  T
G  Y  K  D  L  D  X  O  V  Q  U  E  O  E  W  T  I
M  I  L  V  E  R  T  O  N  R  S  R  N  S  B  I  O
W  Y  Q  B  T  I  E  H  H  U  U  F  P  S  C  L  N
```

Answers on page 189.

WORDS OF A GENIUS

Cryptograms are messages in substitution code. Break the code to read the message. For example, THE SMART CAT might become FVO QWGDF JGF if **F** is substituted for **T**, **V** for **H, O** for **E,** and so on.

BONUS: Who is the speaker of the quote? Which story is the source of the quote?

"ZPO YO YL D JPWLOYGF GM HWOOYFH SWODYAL.
HYRW EW VGPK SWODYAL, DFS MKGE DF DKEBC-
DYK Y TYAA KWOPKF VGP DF WUBWAAWFO WUIWKO
GIYFYGF. ZPO OG KPF CWKW DFS KPF OCWKW, OG
BKGLL-JPWLOYGF KDYATDV HPDKSL, DFS AYW GF
EV MDBW TYOC D AWFL OG EV WVW—YO YL FGO
EV EWOYWK. FG, VGP DKW OCW GFW EDF TCG BDF
BAWDK OCW EDOOWK PI. YM VGP CDRW D MDF-
BV OG LWW VGPK FDEW YF OCW FWUO CGFGPKL
AYLO—"

Answers on page 190.

WHAT CHANGED? (PART I)

The consulting detective was at a house party. What did he see in the toolshed? Examine the objects, then turn the page.

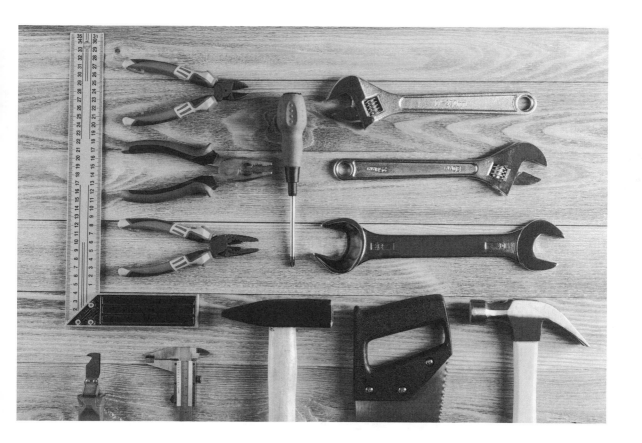

WHAT CHANGED? (PART II)

There was a murder at the house party! The consulting detective immediately spotted that one object changed position, and that object was found to be the hastily cleaned murder weapon. From memory, can you work out what changed position?

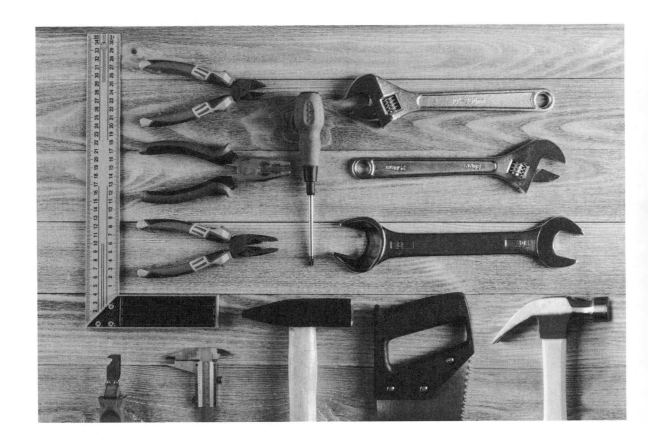

Answer on page 190.

FINGERPRINT MATCH

Find the matching fingerprint(s). There may be more than one.

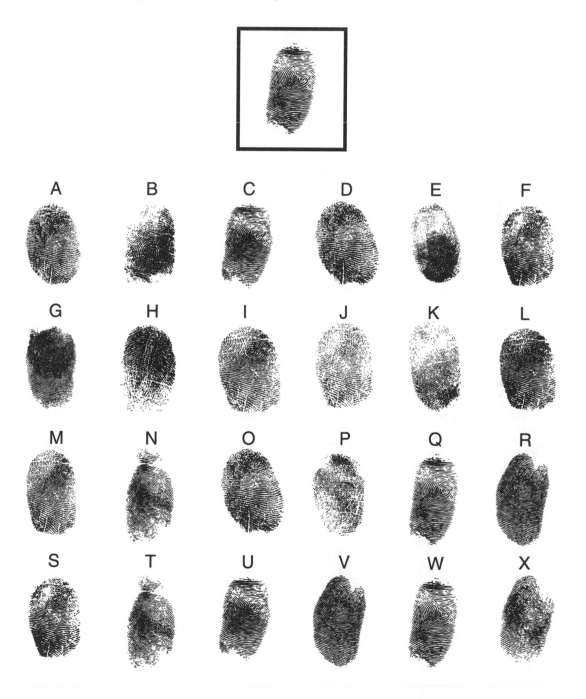

Answers on page 190.

THE MASTER FORGER

The art world is agog! Six recently-sold paintings, each supposed to be by the hand of a different world-famous artist, have now been conclusively shown to be forgeries. Authorities believe the same "master forger" is behind all of this but they're still not sure who he or she actually is. Using only the clues available below, match each forged painting to the artist it was claimed to have been painted by, the country it was sold in, and the price it fetched at auction.

1. The Hal Garrison piece sold for four times as much money as "Cold Hills."

2. "Forever Blue" sold for twice as much as the painting sold in Portugal.

3. Of the piece that sold for $8,000,000 and the Inga Howell painting, one was "Cold Hills" and the other was sold in France.

4. The Inga Howell forgery wasn't sold in Spain.

5. "Baby Jane" (which wasn't passed off as a Margot Lane painting) fetched less money at auction than the piece that was sold in Portugal.

6. Of the painting sold in Germany and "Eighteen," one sold for 32 million dollars and the other was alleged to have been an early work by Greta Frank.

7. The Lyle Kramer painting fetched more money at auction than "Forever Blue," which was said to have been a Hal Garrison piece.

8. "Day of Night," the piece that sold for $2,000,000, and the painting that was sold in Norway were three different forgeries.

9. "Awestruck" didn't sell for either $2 million or $4 million.

10. The Freda Estes painting sold for $16,000,000, but not in Norway.

		Paintings						Countries						Artists					
		Awestruck	Baby Jane	Cold Hills	Day of Night	Eighteen	Forever Blue	Canada	France	Germany	Norway	Portugal	Spain	Freda Estes	Greta Frank	Hal Garrison	Inga Howell	Lyle Kramer	Margot Lane
Prices	$1,000,000																		
	$2,000,000																		
	$4,000,000																		
	$8,000,000																		
	$16,000,000																		
	$32,000,000																		
Artists	Freda Estes																		
	Greta Frank																		
	Hal Garrison																		
	Inga Howell																		
	Lyle Kramer																		
	Margot Lane																		
Countries	Canada																		
	France																		
	Germany																		
	Norway																		
	Portugal																		
	Spain																		

Prices	Paintings	Countries	Artists
$1,000,000			
$2,000,000			
$4,000,000			
$8,000,000			
$16,000,000			
$32,000,000			

157

Answers on page 190.

THE CAT BURGLAR

Maurice St. Clair is considered by many to be the most successful cat burglar of the 20th century. As a local crime reporter, you've been given an assignment to write a story about six of his most daring heists spanning more than 30 years. Using only the clues below, match each of these thefts to the correct month, year, and location, and determine what was stolen in each.

1. The 1991 theft (which wasn't in Seattle) was either the one that happened on July 4th or the one involving the collection of rare blue diamonds.

2. The cash heist, the one in 1998, and the one that took place on April 13th were three different events.

3. Maurice's infamous "Halloween heist" (so-called because it happened on October 31st) didn't involve either diamonds or rubies.

4. Of the cash theft and the Vancouver heist, one happened in July and the other occurred in 1984.

5. The Berlin burglary happened 7 years after the Halloween heist.

6. Of Maurice's 1991 burglary and the one that happened in Paris, one involved blue diamonds and the other occurred on June 15th.

7. The September theft happened sometime after Maurice's infamous London heist.

8. The Seattle heist (which didn't happen in the 1980s) didn't take place in July.

9. The Halloween heist happened 7 years before Maurice's September 10th theft (which involved a large number of pure gold bars).

10. The emerald theft happened sometime before the June 15th heist.

11. The July 4th heist occurred 14 years after the sapphire burglary.

		Cities						Items						Months					
		Antwerp	Berlin	London	Paris	Seattle	Vancouver	Cash	Diamonds	Emeralds	Gold bars	Rubies	Sapphires	April	May	June	July	October	September
Years	1963																		
	1970																		
	1977																		
	1984																		
	1991																		
	1998																		
Months	April																		
	May																		
	June																		
	July																		
	October																		
	September																		
Items	Cash																		
	Diamonds																		
	Emeralds																		
	Gold bars																		
	Rubies																		
	Sapphires																		

Years	Cities	Items	Months
1963			
1970			
1977			
1984			
1991			
1998			

Answers on page 190.

THE FINAL PROBLEM

Each word or phrase in all capitals in the Sherlock Holmes quotation below is contained within the group of letters. Words can be found horizontally, vertically, or diagonally. They may read either forward or backward.

"As you are aware, Watson, there is no one who knows the higher CRIMINAL world of London so well as I do. For years past I have continually been conscious of some POWER behind the MALEFACTOR, some deep organizing power which forever stands in the way of the law, and throws its SHIELD over the WRONG-DOER. Again and again in cases of the most varying sorts— FORGERY cases, ROBBERIES, MURDERS—I have felt the presence of this FORCE, and I have DEDUCED its action in many of those UNDISCOVERED crimes in which I have not been personally CONSULTED. For years I have endeavored to break through the VEIL which SHROUDED it, and at last the time came when I SEIZED my THREAD and followed it, until it led me, after a thousand CUNNING windings, to ex-Professor MORIARTY of MATHEMATICAL celebrity.

"He is the NAPOLEON of crime, Watson. He is the ORGANIZER of half that is EVIL and of nearly all that is UNDETECTED in this great city. He is a GENIUS, a PHILOSOPHER, an abstract thinker. He has a brain of the first order. He sits MOTIONLESS, like a SPIDER in the center of its WEB, but that web has a thousand radiations, and he knows well every QUIVER of each of them. He does little himself. He only PLANS. But his AGENTS are numerous and splendidly organized. Is there a crime to be done, a paper to be ABSTRACTED, we will say, a house to be RIFLED, a man to be removed—the word is passed to the PROFESSOR, the matter is organized and carried out. The agent may be caught. In that case money is found for his BAIL or his defence. But the central power which uses the agent is never caught—never so much as SUSPECTED. This was the organization which I deduced, Watson, and which I DEVOTED my whole energy to EXPOSING and breaking up."

D P W R O N G D O E R J Q V L M L D F
E H S A M O T I O N L E S S A I I E J
T I H G C O N S U L T E D L H G A L W
C L R E U N D I S C O V E R E D B F M
E O O N B Y M D M D J F A R C V C I O
P S U T M T A R R W A B E K E P X R R
S O D S U E Y O H C S C M D I W U C I
U P E Z R L B Y T F R U A O S Q O W A
S H D H B A O N O G U I P X V P P R
E E T H E H R C F O I J I N R L R D T
X R F R R R S W I D E D U C E D O E Y
P S I N S E Q P Y T E L V W H G F T L
O E Q C I U B U L R A V O X E C E C A
S J Z Z I H A G Y A E M O P J B S A N
I H E V S C U N N I N G E T A L S R I
N D E U K W N W L F Y S R H E N O T M
G R O Q O R G A N I Z E R O T D R S I
D L E I H S E L I E V M F A F A F B R
S V A Q E D E T C E T E D N U Z M A C

Answers on page 190.

A "HER LOSS HEMLOCK" ANAGRAM

Below is a quotation from a Sherlock Holmes story. Fill in the blanks in each sentence with a word that is an anagram (rearrangement) of the capitalized word(s).

BONUS: Name the Sherlock Holmes adventure from which this quotation is drawn.

"It is SPICY LIMIT _____ itself," he remarked, chuckling at my surprise, — "so DAY BLURS _____ simple that an explanation is RUEFUL SOUPS _____; and yet it may serve to define the limits of BONSAI TROVE _____ and of DICE DONUT _____. VIBRATE SOON _____ tells me that you have a little reddish mould HI DANGER _____ to your instep. Just PIPE SOOT _____ the Seymour Street Office they have taken up the NAVE TEMP _____ and thrown up some earth which lies in such a way that it is difficult to avoid GRADIENT _____ in it in entering. The earth is of this peculiar HERS DID _____ tint which is found, as far as I know, WHEREON _____ else in the neighborhood. So much is BOA INVESTOR _____. The rest is COD UNTIED _____."

"How, then, did you deduce the RAGE MELT _____?"

"Why, of course I knew that you had not RENT WIT _____ a letter, since I sat opposite to you all GIN NORM _____. I see also in your open desk there that you have a sheet of stamps and a thick bundle of post-cards. What could you go into the post-office for, then, but to send a wire? MAIN ELITE _____ all other FAR COTS _____, and the one which MARINES _____ must be the truth."

Answers on page 191.

WHAT WENT MISSING? (PART I)

The consulting detective met her client in the library about some thefts. Examine the room she saw, then turn the page.

WHAT WENT MISSING? (PART II)

The following day, the client called the consulting detective back about more thefts. The client challenged the consulting detective to spot what had been stolen. From memory, can you work out what went missing?

Answers on page 191.

FAMOUS LAST LINES

How well do you know the Holmes canon? Match the last line of each story to the story's title.

1. "Might I trouble you then to be ready in half an hour, and we can stop at Marcini's for a little dinner on the way?"

2. The famous air-gun of Von Herder will embellish the Scotland Yard Museum, and once again Mr. Sherlock Holmes is free to devote his life to examining those interesting little problems which the complex life of London so plentifully presents.

3. "If ever you write an account, Watson, you can make rabbits serve your turn."

4. "Watson, I think our quiet rest in the country has been a distinct success, and I shall certainly return much invigorated to Baker Street to-morrow."

5. "Draw your chair up and hand me my violin, for the only problem we have still to solve is how to while away these bleak autumnal evenings."

A. The Adventure of the Noble Bachelor

B. The Adventure of the Empty House

C. The Adventure of the Norwood Builder

D. The Adventure of the Reigate Puzzle (or the Reigate Squire)

E. The Hound of the Baskervilles

Answers on page 191.

THE CON ARTIST

The F.B.I. has been on the hunt for a con artist accused of swindling thousands of dollars from his victims. His real name is Barney Green, but he routinely jumps from place to place using a new assumed name whenever he moves to a new location. Barney always creates a new fake "career" for each of his identities, and he never kept the same identity for more than a month. Help the F.B.I. track Mr. Green's latest movements by matching each name he used to its correct location and month, and determine the "career" he invented for each fake identity.

1. Of the "Fred Flores" identity and whichever name Barney used in Trippany, one was supposedly a doctor and the other was used in July.

2. Mr. Green didn't pass himself off as a lawyer while he was using the name "Pat Perry."

3. Barney pretended to be an accountant one month and a bank manager during another. One of those two identities was "Abe Avery". The other was the one he used in June.

4. He pretended to be "Sean Starr" sometime after he passed himself off as an accountant.

5. The F.B.I. know two of Barney's fake names were "Abe Avery" and "Matt Mintz," and that of those two, he used one in the city of Valero and he used the other in May.

6. Barney was in the town of Hoople either in August or in whichever month he pretended to be a dentist (but not both).

7. Mr. Green claimed to be a reporter one month before he was in Beaverton. Sometime after he left Beaverton he used the name "Pat Perry".

8. We know for a fact that Barney was pretending to be a doctor during his time in Opalville, and that he was in Nanaimo in May.

9. He never used the name "Lou Lemon" during his time in Beaverton, and he didn't pass himself off as an accountant in April.

	Names						Towns						Careers					
	Abe Avery	Fred Flores	Lou Lemon	Matt Mintz	Pat Perry	Sean Starr	Beaverton	Hoople	Nanaimo	Opalville	Trippany	Valero	Accountant	Bank mgr.	Dentist	Doctor	Lawyer	Reporter
March																		
April																		
May																		
June																		
July																		
August																		
Accountant																		
Bank mgr.																		
Dentist																		
Doctor																		
Lawyer																		
Reporter																		
Beaverton																		
Hoople																		
Nanaimo																		
Opalville																		
Trippany																		
Valero																		

Months	Names	Towns	Careers
March			
April			
May			
June			
July			
August			

Answers on page 191.

A "SHH MOLE LOCKER" ANAGRAM

Below is a quotation from a Sherlock Holmes story. Fill in the blanks in each sentence with a word that is an anagram (rearrangement) of the capitalized word(s).

BONUS: Name the Sherlock Holmes adventure from which this quotation is drawn.

"You will remember that I remarked the other day, just before we went into the very IMPELS _____ problem presented by Miss Mary Sutherland, that for strange effects and ERRATA RID ONYX _____ combinations we must go to life itself, which is always far more AD RING _____ than any effort of the I GO MAINTAIN _____."

"A proposition which I took the BILE TRY _____ of BIND GOUT _____."

"You did, COT ROD _____, but none the less you must come round to my view, for otherwise I shall keep on GIN LIP _____ fact upon fact on you until your reason breaks down under them and WACKO LEGENDS _____ me to be right. Now, Mr. Jabez Wilson here has been good enough to call upon me this morning, and to begin a RAVINE RAT _____ which promises to be one of the most SLAG RUIN _____ which I have listened to for some time. You have heard me remark that the ANGST REST _____ and most unique things are very often DECENT CON _____ not with the larger but with the smaller MRS ICE _____, and occasionally, indeed, where there is room for doubt whether any TOP IVIES _____ crime has been committed. As far as I have heard it is MOBILE SIPS _____ for me to say whether the present case is an ANCIENTS _____ of crime or not, but the course of events is CLEAR TINY _____ among the most SNUG LIAR _____ that I have ever listened to."

Answers on page 192.

WHAT WENT MISSING? (PART I)

The consulting detective was at a house party. What did he see in the toolshed? Examine the objects, then turn the page.

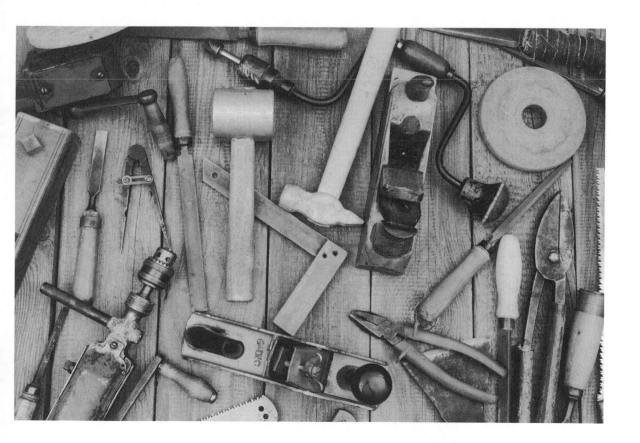

WHAT WENT MISSING? (PART II)

There was a murder at the house party! The consulting detective immediately spotted that one object disappeared, and was possibly the murder weapon. From memory, can you work out what went missing?

170

Answers on page 192.

ANSWERS

A "Sol Ohm Hecklers" Anagram
(page 4)

"Really, Watson, you excel YOURSELF," said Holmes, pushing back his chair and lighting a cigarette. "I am bound to say that in all the ACCOUNTS which you have been so good as to give of my own small ACHIEVEMENTS you have habitually UNDERRATED your own abilities. It may be that you are not yourself LUMINOUS, but you are a conductor of light. Some people without POSSESS-ING genius have a remarkable power of STIMULATING it. I confess, my dear FELLOW, that I am very much in your debt."

BONUS ANSWER: "The Hound of the Baskervilles"

A Study in Sherlock
(page 5)

1. A; 2. C; 3. B; 4. A; 5. C

For Stage and Screen
(page 6)

D	O	N	A	L	D	P	I	C	K	E	R	I	N	G
A	K	K	B	N	B	R	U	C	E	M	C	R	A	E
V	R	A	Y	M	O	N	D	F	R	A	N	C	I	S
I	Q	Y	X	O	C	N	A	L	A	Q	Q	Y	R	R
D	G	N	U	O	Y	D	N	A	L	O	R	W	O	F
B	E	N	K	I	N	G	S	L	E	Y	H	F	B	B
U	I	N	I	G	E	L	B	R	U	C	E	X	E	V
R	T	R	H	T	F	Q	S	C	D	Q	J	S	R	M
K	W	P	O	J	X	D	Y	R	Y	U	V	I	T	H
E	K	C	I	W	D	R	A	H	D	R	A	W	D	E
M	A	R	T	I	N	F	R	E	E	M	A	N	U	I
W	E	L	L	E	B	E	L	R	Y	K	H	C	V	T
H	X	E	E	N	C	A	M	K	C	I	R	T	A	P
S	I	L	L	I	W	T	R	E	B	U	H	M	L	V
W	J	M	C	O	L	I	N	B	L	A	K	E	L	Y

Fingerprint Match
(page 8)

The matching pairs are: A and G; B and H; C and E; D and F

What Went Missing?
(Part I) (page 9)

See part II.

What Went Missing?
(Part II) (page 10)
The chess set. When the client and chess set were found, it turned out the diamond was hidden in one of the pieces.

ANSWERS

For His Generation
(page 11)

Jeremy Brett played the sleuth in a long-running television series produced by Granada Television in the eighties and nineties. Forty-two of Arthur Conan Doyle's stories were adapted for the series, and the series had a reputation for being faithful to the books. Brett had actually played Watson in 1980, across from Charlton Heston's Holmes.

Nothing to Do with Doyle
(page 11)

H.H. Holmes wasn't a fictional detective—he was a serial killer, often considered the first in America. Born Herman Webster Mudgett in 1861, he confessed to 27 murders but may have been responsible for more. He was also a bigamist, married to three women at the time of his death.

Art Thefts
(pages 12-13)

Months	Titles	Artists	Museums
April	City Dreams	De Lorenzo	Givernelle
May	Apple Cart	Strauss	Tendrille
June	Elba at Dawn	Pocalini	Beaufort
July	Madame V.	Lafayette	Millefoi

Interception
(page 14)

Take the last letter of each place name to reveal: CHICAGO

A "Shh Cello Smoker" Anagram
(page 15)

"No, no. No crime," said Sherlock Holmes, laughing. "Only one of those WHIMSICAL little INCIDENTS which will happen when you have four million human beings all JOSTLING each other within the space of a few square miles. Amid the action and reaction of so dense a swarm of HUMANITY, every possible COMBINATION of events may be expected to take place, and many a little problem will be presented which may be STRIKING and BIZARRE without being criminal. We have ALREADY had experience of such."

BONUS ANSWER: "The Adventure of the Blue Carbuncle"

The Hound of the Baskervilles
(pages 16-17)

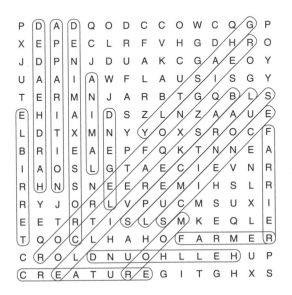

ANSWERS

Crack the Password
(page 18)

The missing letter is O.
noise, primrose, loaner, mosaic

In Other Words
(page 18)

Synonyms for mysterious include secret, enigmatic, furtive, shadowy, cryptic, and clandestine.

What Went Missing?
(Part I) (page 19)

See part II.

What Went Missing?
(Part II) (page 20)

All the books on the top right shelf have gone missing. The documents were hidden in one of them.

Famous First Lines
(page 21)

1. C; 2. D; 3. A; 4. B. 5. E

The Missing Millionaire
(pages 22-23)

Days	Witnesses	Cities	States
Tuesday	Edna Eddel	Ballingford	Nevada
Wednesday	Hilda Hayes	Tetley	California
Thursday	Susie Seuss	Ventura	Washington
Friday	Walt Wolsen	Pescadero	Oregon

A "Smell Oh Shocker" Anagram
(page 24)

I had neither kith nor kin in England, and was therefore as free as Air—or as free as an INCOME of eleven shillings and sixpence a day will PERMIT a man to be. Under such circumstances, I naturally gravitated to London, that great CESSPOOL into which all the LOUNGERS and idlers of the Empire are irresistibly drained. There I stayed for some time at a PRIVATE hotel in the Strand, leading a COMFORTLESS, meaningless existence, and spending such money as I had, considerably more FREELY than I ought. So ALARMING did the state of my FINANCES become, that I soon realized that I must either leave the metropolis and RUSTICATE somewhere in the country, or that I must make a complete ALTERATION in my style of living. Choosing the latter alternative, I began by making up my mind to leave the hotel, and to take up my quarters in some less PRETENTIOUS and less expensive DOMICILE.

BONUS ANSWER: "A Study in Scarlet"

What the Consulting Detective Saw (Part I) (page 25)

See part II.

ANSWERS

What the Consulting Detective Saw (Part II) (page 26)

Picture 3 is a match.

Everybody and His Brother

(page 27)

Actor Christopher Lee played the famous detective in the 1962 movie "Sherlock Holmes and the Deadly Necklace." In 1970, Lee played a Holmes again—Sherlock's brother Mycroft, in the movie "The Private Life of Sherlock Holmes." He had also played Sir Henry Baskerville in an earlier film adapted from "The Hound of the Baskervilles."

For His Generation

(page 27)

One of the most famous portrayals of Holmes came from Basil Rathbone in the Forties. Rathbone played the detective in fourteen films. Earlier films were set in Victorian times, while some of the later installations were set in the Forties, with plots related to the second World War. There was also a radio series.

The Empty House

(pages 28-29)

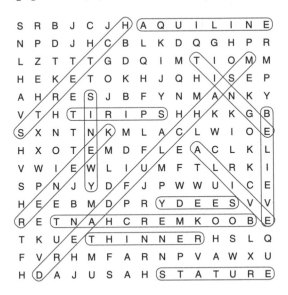

Celebrating Sherlock

(page 30)

The Baker Street stop on the London Underground has tiles that show the silhouette of the most famous (if fictional) resident of that street. Nearby is a museum devoted to the man and his work.

Crack the Password

(page 30)

The missing letter is S.
monster, passion, relapse, scullery

What Went Missing?

(Part I) (page 31)

See part II.

174

ANSWERS

What Went Missing?
(Part II) (page 32)

The frame above the mantelpiece disappeared (the documents were taped to the back of it).

What the Consulting Detective
Saw (Part I) (page 33)

See part 2.

What the Consulting Detective
Saw (Part II) (page 34)

Picture 2 is a match.

Tracking the Hound of the
Baskervilles (page 35)

1. B; 2. A 3. B; 4. C; 5. B

Passing Bad Checks
(pages 36-37)

Dates	Stores	Towns	Amounts
October 2	Carpet City	Rio Pondo	$125.12
October 6	Well Mart	Georgetown	$85.50
October 10	Quick-Stop	Appleton	$52.89
October 14	David's Deli	Lincoln	$35.15

The Women of Sherlock
Holmes (pages 38-39)

A "Clerks Shoo Helm" Anagram
(page 40)

"My dear fellow," said Sherlock Holmes as we sat on either side of the fire in his LODGINGS at Baker Street, "life is INFINITELY stranger than anything which the mind of man could INVENT. We would not dare to CONCEIVE the things which are really mere COMMONPLACES of existence. If we could fly out of that WINDOW hand in hand, hover over this great city, gently REMOVE the roofs, and peep in at the queer things which are going on, the strange COIN-CIDENCES, the plannings, the cross-purposes, the WONDERFUL chains of events, working through GENERATIONS, and leading to the most outré results, it would make all fiction with its conventionalities and FORESEEN conclusions most stale and UNPROFITABLE."

BONUS ANSWER: "A Case of Identity"

ANSWERS

What Went Missing?
(Part I) (page 41)

See part II.

What Went Missing?
(Part II) (page 42)

One of the couch pillows went missing (the documents were stuffed inside).

What the Consulting Detective Saw (Part I) (page 43)

See part 2.

What the Consulting Detective Saw (Part II) (page 44)

Picture 3 is a match.

Interception
(page 45)

Take the central letter of each word and you reveal LONDON.

The Escape Artist
(pages 46-47)

Years	Prisons	States	Methods
2001	Middle Fork	Alabama	wire cutters
2005	Tulveride	Idaho	uniform
2009	Pennington	Montana	tunnel
2013	Lexington	Virginia	ladder
2017	Calahatchee	Colorado	rope

Famous First Lines
(page 48)

1. B; 2. D; 3. E; 4. A; 5. C

Fingerprint Match
(page 49)

The matching pairs are: A and K; B and I; C and L; D and J; E and H; F and N; G and P; M and O

The "Gloria Scott"
(pages 50-51)

I N P Q G P P V N O M J E L L
G T N E D I C C A A B C E Y B
Y T I L A T I P S O H P I U V
F E N C I N G N X T A P L K A
L I Q R L O Z I H H I L T H C
R G U U X Z N S C C T S H Y A
I F I M Z G V F Z E S U I W T
C E R O V E R T R O T C I V I
O L E P T I U R C T Z S Y G O
L L R I E S I I V D Y I U B N
L O Z N Q E A H U D A N K L E
E W D G R B O Z U U N I O N E
G S H C L M E T H O D S Y W T
E Q V E F J S P R O S A I C Z
M E T I S O P P O D C S V H G

ANSWERS

A Surprising Viewpoint
(page 52)

"I consider that a man's brain originally is like a little empty attic, and you have to stock it with such furniture as you choose. A fool takes in all the lumber of every sort that he comes across, so that the knowledge which might be useful to him gets crowded out, or at best is jumbled up with a lot of other things so that he has a difficulty in laying his hands upon it. Now the skilful workman is very careful indeed as to what he takes into his brain-attic. He will have nothing but the tools which may help him in doing his work, but of these he has a large assortment, and all in the most perfect order. It is a mistake to think that that little room has elastic walls and can distend to any extent. Depend upon it there comes a time when for every addition of knowledge you forget something that you knew before. It is of the highest importance, therefore, not to have useless facts elbowing out the useful ones."

BONUS ANSWER: Sherlock Holmes is the speaker in "A Study in Scarlet"

What Went Missing?
(Part I) (page 53)

See part II.

What Went Missing?
(Part II) (page 54)

The lipstick went missing.

In Cap and Cape
(page 55)

Doyle's stories were serialized in a magazine called The Strand, and accompanied by illustrations created by Sidney Paget. The idea that Holmes wore a deerstalker cap and an Inverness cape comes not directly from Doyle but from Paget's illustrations. Paget had two brothers, both illustrators; by one account, brother Walter was originally intended to do the first illustrations, but the publishers sent the letter to Sidney instead.

An Enduring Trait
(page 56)

The detective's signature calabash pipe was popularized by William Gillette, who played Holmes on stage in the late 1800s and early 1900s. Sidney Paget's illustrations showed the sleuth with a straight pipe, but Gillette used a curvy calabash pipe, a detail that lasted in the decades that followed.

Crack the Password
(page 56)

The missing letter is L.
amoral, central, flamingo, musical

What Went Missing?
(Part I) (page 57)

See part II.

ANSWERS

What Went Missing?
(Part II) (page 58)

The pair of scissors went missing.

A "Oh Shell Mockers" Anagram
(page 59)

"CIRCUMSTANTIAL EVIDENCE is a very tricky thing," answered Holmes thoughtfully. "It may seem to point very STRAIGHT to one thing, but if you shift your own point of view a little, you may find it pointing in an equally UNCOMPROMISING manner to something entirely different. It must be confessed, however, that the case looks EXCEEDINGLY grave against the young man, and it is very possible that he is indeed the CULPRIT. There are several people in the neighbourhood, however, and among them Miss Turner, the daughter of the neighbouring LANDOWNER, who believe in his INNOCENCE, and who have RETAINED Lestrade, whom you may recollect in connection with the Study in SCARLET, to work out the case in his interest. Lestrade, being rather puzzled, has REFERRED the case to me, and hence it is that two middle-aged GENTLEMEN are flying WESTWARD at fifty miles an hour instead of quietly DIGESTING their BREAKFASTS at home."

BONUS ANSWER: "The Boscombe Valley Mystery"

The Musgrave Ritual
(pages 60-61)

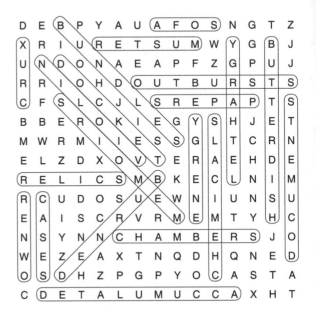

The Suspect List
(pages 62-63)

Ages	Suspects	Professions	Towns
23	Vincent	lawyer	Midvale
26	Michael	engineer	Flagstaff
29	Nicholas	tennis pro	Billings
32	Albert	architect	Tulverton
35	Dennis	dentist	San Pedro

Interception
(page 64)

Take the second letter of each word and you reveal: BUCHAREST

ANSWERS

What the Consulting Detective Saw
(Part I) (page 65)

See part 2.

What the Consulting Detective Saw
(Part II) (page 66)

1. Two, numbered 1 and 4; 2. Wineglass; 3. Fork; 4. True; 5. True

Rental Agreements
(page 67)

Not only was her first-floor flat invaded at all hours by throngs of singular and often undesirable characters but her remarkable lodger showed an eccentricity and irregularity in his life which must have sorely tried her patience. His incredible untidiness, his addiction to music at strange hours, his occasional revolver practice within doors, his weird and often malodorous scientific experiments, and the atmosphere of violence and danger which hung around him made him the very worst tenant in London. On the other hand, his payments were princely.

BONUS ANSWER: Mrs. Hudson and Sherlock Holmes are described in "The Adventure of the Dying Detective"

Telephone Records
(pages 68-69)

Times	People	Numbers	Lengths
1:52am	Kerry	239-4827	22 seconds
1:57am	Charlie	447-6995	3 minutes
2:02am	Vicky	731-9262	48 seconds
2:07am	Mitchell	592-0021	35 seconds
2:12am	Sarah	368-7841	1.5 minutes

The Adventure of the Resident Patient (page 70)

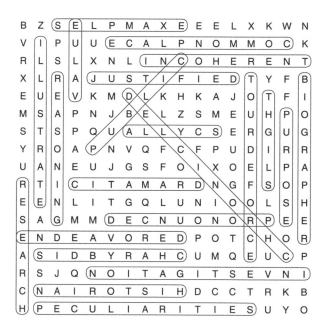

ANSWERS

A "Lock Helm Horses" Anagram
(page 72)

He was a man of about fifty, tall, PORTLY, and imposing, with a massive, strongly marked face and a COMMANDING figure. He was dressed in a sombre yet rich style, in black FROCK-COAT, shining hat, neat brown GAITERS, and well-cut pearl-grey TROUSERS. Yet his actions were in absurd contrast to the DIGNITY of his dress and features, for he was running hard, with OCCASIONAL little springs, such as a weary man gives who is little ACCUSTOMED to set any tax upon his legs. As he ran he jerked his hands up and down, waggled his head, and WRITHED his face into the most extraordinary CONTORTIONS.

BONUS ANSWER: "The Adventure of the Beryl Coronet"

What Went Missing?
(Part I) (page 73)

See part II.

What Went Missing?
(Part II) (page 74)

The hand spade went missing.

A Seeker of Truth
(page 75)

In the 1930s, Bengali writer Sharadindu Bandyopadhyay introduced a character named Byomkesh Bakshi, who solved mysteries but preferred the term "truth-seeker" to detective. The character appeared in 32 stories in the decades that followed, and inspired a television show and several movies. He's been called "The Indian Sherlock Holmes."

Crack the Password
(page 75)

The missing letter is P.
clapper, desperate, flipper, input

Grave Robberies
(pages 76-77)

Dates	Cemeteries	Graves	Towns
March 12th	Box Grove	Brad Beaudry	Verona
March 20th	Apple Pine	Ruben Yates	Upperdale
March 28th	Green Lawn	Pat Fowler	Shell City
April 5th	Calvary Cape	Holden Bray	Wilmette
April 13th	Dinby Dale	Ed Lowder	Trenton

Famous Last Lines
(page 78)

Answers: 1. D; 2. C; 3. A; 4. B. 5. E

ANSWERS

Duality
(page 79)

Many actors have played Holmes, and many have played Watson—but British actor Patrick Macnee was one of the few to play both roles during a long career! He played the character of Watson opposite Roger Moore and Christopher Lee. And to cap it off, in 1984, he played a character on the television show Magnum P.I. who had a delusion that he was Sherlock Holmes.

The Adventure of the Greek Interpreter **(pages 80-81)**

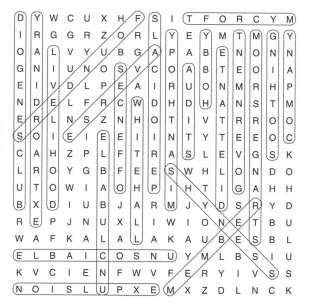

A "Mocks Shell Hero" Anagram
(page 82)

"Pshaw, my dear fellow, what do the public, the great UNOBSERVANT public, who could hardly tell a WEAVER by his tooth or a compositor by his left thumb, care about the finer shades of ANALYSIS and deduction! But, indeed, if you are TRIVIAL, I cannot blame you, for the days of the great cases are past. Man, or at least criminal man, has lost all ENTERPRISE and ORIGINALITY. As to my own little practice, it seems to be DEGENERATING into an agency for recovering lost lead pencils and giving ADVICE to young ladies from boarding-schools. I think that I have touched bottom at last, however. This note I had this morning marks my zero-point, I fancy. Read it!" He tossed a CRUMPLED letter across to me.

BONUS ANSWER: "The Adventure of the Copper Beeches"

What Went Missing?
(Part I) (page 83)

See part II.

What Went Missing?
(Part II) (page 84)

The brace went missing.

ANSWERS

Another Resident of Baker Street
(page 85)

In the television show House, the title character, Gregory House, was partly inspired by and has many characteristics in common with the fictional detective even though the mysteries he solved were medical instead of criminal. Shore, the show's creator, was a big fan. House, like his predecessor, was irascible, had a companion (James Wilson instead of John Watson), and even lived on Baker Street! The names House, in fact, sounds like "homes," a homonym of the detective's name.

Witness Statements
(pages 86-87)

Heights	Witnesses	Weights	Cars
5' 2"	Russell T.	190 lbs	Chevrolet
5' 5"	Sarah M.	145 lbs	Toyota
5' 8"	Yolanda V.	135 lbs	Honda
5' 11"	Angela S.	225 lbs	Mazda
6' 2"	Gerald F.	160 lbs	Nissan

Fingerprint Match
(page 88)

H is the matching fingerprint.

What Changed?
(Part I) (page 89)

See part II.

What Changed?
(Part II) (page 90)

The frying pan flipped.

What the Consulting Detective Saw
(Part I) (page 91)

See part II.

What the Consulting Detective Saw (Part II) (page 92)

Picture 4 is a match.

A "Hello Her Smocks" Anagram
(page 93)

"It is one of those cases where the art of the REASONER should be used rather for the SIFTING of DETAILS than for the acquiring of fresh EVIDENCE. The tragedy has been so uncommon, so complete and of such PERSONAL importance to so many people, that we are suffering from a PLETHORA of surmise, conjecture, and HYPOTHESIS. The difficulty is to DETACH the framework of fact—of absolute UNDENIABLE fact—from the embellishments of THEORISTS and reporters. Then, having established ourselves upon this sound basis, it is our duty to see what INFERENCES may be drawn and what are the SPECIAL points upon which the whole mystery turns."

BONUS ANSWER: "The Adventure of Silver Blaze"

International Fugitives (pages 94-95)

Dates	Criminals	Crimes	Countries
October 3	Grendle	robbery	Peru
October 4	Dornmer	forgery	Moldova
October 5	Filcher	tax evasion	France
October 6	Blackforth	arson	Uganda
October 7	Calumnet	blackmail	Sweden

ANSWERS

Interception
(page 96)

Take the central letter of each word and you get ALINAM. Flip this, and it becomes MANILA

A Study in Sherlock
(page 97)

1. Nil; 2. Nil; 3. Nil; 4. Feeble; 5. Variable (Watson further describes his botanical knowledge as "Well up in belladonna, opium, and poisons generally. Knows nothing of practical gardening."); 6. Practical, but limited. 7. Profound; 8. Accurate, but unsystematic; 9. Immense.

Anna's Alibis
(pages 98-99)

Times	Alibis	Relations	Locations
8:00pm	Penny Pugh	neighbor	Delancey Rd.
8:30pm	Lina Lopez	friend	First St.
9:00pm	Norma Neet	co-worker	Ewing Ave.
9:30pm	Maddy Meyer	bartender	Capitol St.
10:00pm	Oda Osborn	cousin	Border Ln.

The Adventure of the Norwood Builder (pages 100-101)

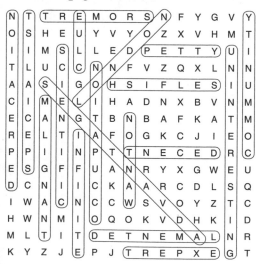

A "Hock Meshes Roll" Anagram
(page 102)

"It is not cold which makes me shiver," said the woman in a low voice, changing her seat as REQUESTED.
"What, then?"
"It is fear, Mr. Holmes. It is TERROR." She raised her veil as she spoke, and we could see that she was indeed in a PITIABLE state of AGITATION, her face all drawn and grey, with restless FRIGHTENED eyes, like those of some hunted animal. Her FEATURES and figure were those of a woman of thirty, but her hair was shot with PREMATURE grey, and her expression was weary and HAGGARD. Sherlock Holmes ran her over with one of his quick, all-comprehensive glances.
"You must not fear," said he SOOTHINGLY, bending forward and patting her FOREARM. "We shall soon set matters right, I have no DOUBT. You have come in by TRAIN this morning, I see."

BONUS ANSWER: "The Adventure of the Speckled Band"

What Went Missing?
(Part I) (page 103)

See part II.

What Went Missing?
(Part II) (page 104)

The keys went missing.

ANSWERS

A Sad Statistic
(page 105)

The percentage of stolen art that is recovered is not very high. Only five to ten percent might be recovered.

A Mysterious Event
(page 105)

The year 1911 involved a notable case of art theft—the Mona Lisa was stolen from the Louvre by an employee. He was caught two years later and the painting was returned to its home.

Marked Bills
(pages 106-107)

Dates	Serials	Locations	Denominations
April 1	G-718428	Torbin	$50
April 5	F-667280	Midvale	$100
April 9	B-492841	Uteville	$5
April 13	C-918303	Nettleton	$10
April 17	P-101445	Finsberg	$20

Bank Robberies
(pages 108-109)

Dates	Banks	Towns	Amounts
June 3	First Trust	Longwood	$1,000
June 5	Moneycorp	Yountville	$1,600
June 7	Wellspring	Tahoe	$4,800
June 9	Bell Largo	Grumley	$2,500
June 11	Apex	Cold Spring	$10,200

The Adventure of Black Peter
(pages 110-111)

Thinking Things Through (page 112)

"There are two questions waiting for us at the outset. The one is whether any crime has been committed at all; the second is, what is the crime and how was it committed? Of course, if Dr. Mortimer's surmise should be correct, and we are dealing with forces outside the ordinary laws of Nature, there is an end of our investigation. But we are bound to exhaust all other hypotheses before falling back upon this one. I think we'll shut that window again, if you don't mind. It is a singular thing, but I find that a concentrated atmosphere helps a concentration of thought. I have not pushed it to the length of getting into a box to think, but that is the logical outcome of my convictions."

BONUS ANSWER: Sherlock Holmes in "The Hound of the Baskervilles"

ANSWERS

What Went Missing?
(Part I) (page 113)

See part II.

What Went Missing?
(Part II) (page 114)

The nail polish went missing.

Interception
(page 115)

Take the first letter and the last letter of each word to reveal: WASHINGTON DC

Rare Wines (pages 116-117)

Vintages	Wines	Types	Countries
1954	Weimerund	syrah	Italy
1958	Ania Branco	pinot noir	Spain
1962	Friambliss	pinot gris	Portugal
1966	Ece Suss	chardonnay	Greece
1970	Vendemmia	merlot	France

Describing Sherlock Holmes
(page 118)

"It is not easy to express the inexpressible," he answered with a laugh. "Holmes is a little too scientific for my tastes—it approaches to cold-bloodedness. I could imagine his giving a friend a little pinch of the latest vegetable alkaloid, not out of malevolence, you understand, but simply out of a spirit of inquiry in order to have an accurate idea of the effects. To do him justice, I think that he would take it himself with the same readiness. He appears to have a passion for definite and exact knowledge."

BONUS ANSWER: The character of Stamford, in "A Study in Scarlet"

What the Consulting Detective Saw (Part I) (page 119)

See part II.

What the Consulting Detective Saw (Part II) (page 120)

Picture 4 is a match.

Fingerprint Match
(page 121)

The matching pairs are: A and S; B and V; C and P; D and M; E and O; F and G; H and T; I and R; J and X; K and W; L and U; N and Q

ANSWERS

The Adventure of the Golden Pince-Nez (pages 122-123)

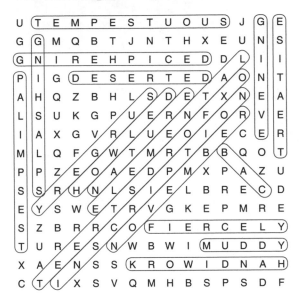

Smuggled Electronics (pages 124-125)

Departures	Flights	Gates	Items
8:03am	108	11	watches
8:10am	233	18	televisions
8:17am	356	3	tablets
8:24am	510	6	cell phones
8:31am	92	7	laptops

A "Cork Shell Homes" Anagram (page 126)

Sherlock Holmes was a man who seldom took EXERCISE for EXERCISE'S sake. Few men were capable of greater MUSCULAR effort, and he was UNDOUBTEDLY one of the finest boxers of his WEIGHT that I have ever seen; but he looked upon aimless bodily EXERTION as a waste of energy, and he seldom BESTIRRED himself save when there was some professional object to be served. Then he was absolutely UNTIRING and INDEFATIGABLE. That he should have kept himself in TRAINING under such CIRCUMSTANCES is remarkable, but his diet was usually of the SPAREST, and his habits were simple to the verge of AUSTERITY.

BONUS ANSWER: "The Adventure of the Yellow Face"

What Changed? (Part I) (page 127)

See part II.

What Changed? (Part II) (page 128)

They flipped the labels on Iodum and Arnica.

Fill in the Empty House (page 129)

1. B; 2. A; 3. A; 4. C; 5. B

ANSWERS

For Stage and Screen
(page 130-131)

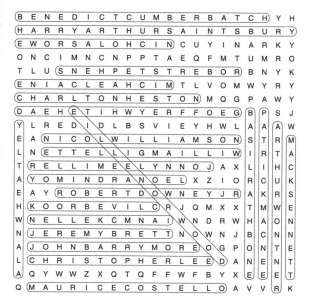

A "Ms Holler Chokes" Anagram
(page 132)

"Porlock, Watson, is a NOM-DE-PLUME, a mere identification mark; but behind it lies a shifty and EVASIVE personality. In a former letter he FRANKLY informed me that the name was not his own, and DEFIED me ever to trace him among the TEEMING millions of this great city. Porlock is important, not for HIMSELF, but for the great man with whom he is in touch. PICTURE to yourself the pilot fish with the SHARK, the jackal with the lion—anything that is insignificant in companionship with what is FORMIDABLE: not only FORMIDABLE, Watson, but SINISTER—in the highest degree SINISTER. That is where he comes within my purview. You have heard me speak of PROFESSOR MORIARTY?"

BONUS ANSWER: "The Valley of Fear"

What the Consulting Detective Saw
(Part I) (page 133)

See part II.

What the Consulting Detective Saw
(Part II) (page 134)

Picture 1 is a match.

What Went Missing?
(Part I) (page 135)

See part II.

What Went Missing?
(Part II) (page 136)

The row of four serving spoons went missing.

ANSWERS

A "Shh Cooker Smell" Anagram
(page 137)

It was difficult to REFUSE any of Sherlock Holmes' requests, for they were always so exceedingly DEFINITE, and put forward with such a quiet air of MASTERY. I felt, however, that when Whitney was once CONFINED in the cab my mission was practically AC-COMPLISHED; and for the rest, I could not wish anything better than to be ASSOCI-ATED with my friend in one of those singular ADVENTURES which were the normal condition of his EXISTENCE. In a few minutes I had written my note, paid Whitney's bill, led him out to the cab, and seen him driven through the DARKNESS. In a very short time a DECREPIT figure had emerged from the OPIUM DEN, and I was walking down the street with Sherlock Holmes. For two streets he SHUFFLED along with a bent back and an UNCERTAIN foot. Then, glancing quickly round, he straightened himself out and burst into a HEARTY fit of laughter.

BONUS ANSWER: "The Man with the Twisted Lip"

Stolen Street Signs
(page 138)

Dates	Signs	Streets	Streets
July 4th	One Way	Dwight St.	Ralston Ave.
July 11th	Speed Limit	Casper Blvd.	Tarragon Ln.
July 18th	Dead End	Amble Ln.	Quinella St.
July 25th	Yield	Barnacle Rd.	Selby St.
August 1st	Stop	Falstaff St.	Oracle Rd.
August 8th	No Parking	Everett Ave.	Peabody Ln.

The Reigate Puzzle
(page 140)

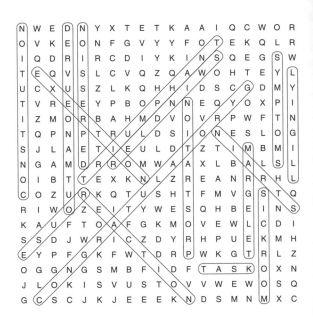

Famous First Lines (page 142)

1. E; 2. C; 3. D; 4. A. 5. B

What Went Missing?
(Part I) (page 143)

See part II.

What Went Missing?
(Part II) (page 144)

The canister of film had been stolen.

ANSWERS

Stop, Thief!
(page 145)

Did you know that the famous detective lost his first case? His first case on film, that is. In 1900, a short silent film called, "Sherlock Holmes Baffled," was created. In the film, an intruder repeatedly comes into frame and steals from the sleuth. As promised in the title, the burglar gets away unscathed. Of course, the film only runs thirty seconds, so perhaps justice would have prevailed if the filmstrip had continued.

Interception
(page 146)

Take the central letter of each word in the phrase and you get: ESUOHEFAS, CED, TSRIF,MPENO. Read each item backwards and you get: safehouse, Dec. first, One PM.

What Changed?
(Part I) (page 147)

See part II.

What Changed?
(Part II) (page 148)

The meat fork was flipped.

A "Chrome Elk Slosh" Anagram
(page 149)

To Sherlock Holmes she is always THE woman. I have seldom heard him MENTION her under any other name. In his eyes she ECLIPSES and predominates the whole of her sex. It was not that he felt any EMOTION akin to love for Irene Adler. All EMOTIONS, and that one particularly, were ABHORRENT to his cold, precise but admirably BALANCED mind. He was, I take it, the most perfect reasoning and observing MACHINE that the world has seen, but as a lover he would have placed himself in a false POSITION. He never spoke of the softer PASSIONS, save with a gibe and a sneer. They were ADMIRABLE things for the observer—excellent for drawing the veil from men's MOTIVES and actions. But for the trained reasoner to admit such INTRUSTIONS into his own delicate and finely adjusted TEMPERAMENT was to introduce a distracting factor which might throw a doubt upon all his mental results. Grit in a sensitive INSTRUMENT, or a crack in one of his own high-power lenses, would not be more DISTURBING than a strong emotion in a nature such as his. And yet there was but one woman to him, and that woman was the late Irene Adler, of dubious and QUESTIONABLE memory.

BONUS ANSWER: "A Scandal in Bohemia"

Charles Augustus Milverton
(pages 150-151)

```
H N D V J B S U O M O N E V M Y T
C S M I L I N G Q N S K Q R A E U
T R S G H J G Y E A R O M O R F E
R U E D L S S Q U E E Z E C B K N
A R R E L I F Z G Z L W E P L S K
E Q P C P M D E T Z I S Z D E R F
H Y E B S I E I K P A W I C K E D
Q S N U A P N F N W M N N F R R R
E L T K V G I G D G K O V P E E E
S I S U N B A X Y J C I I B W D P
R T L H P B R G E K A S T U O R U
K H P E E M D G I G L L A S P U T
I E J O L E F B G L B U T I R M A
N R D H A B A H P M W P I N A B T
G Y K D L D X O V Q U E O E W T I
M I L V E R T O N R S R N S B I O
W Y Q B T I E H H U U F P S C L N
```

189

Words of a Genius
(page 152)

"But it is a question of getting details. Give me your details, and from an armchair I will return you an excellent expert opinion. But to run here and run there, to cross-question railway guards, and lie on my face with a lens to my eye—it is not my metier. No, you are the one man who can clear the matter up. If you have a fancy to see your name in the next honours list—"

BONUS ANSWER: The speaker is Mycroft Holmes in "The Adventure of the Bruce-Partington Plans"

What Changed?
(Part I) (page 153)

See part II.

What Changed?
(Part II) (page 154)

The hammer changed positons.

Fingerprint Match
(page 155)

Q and W are the matching fingerprints.

The Master Forger
(pages 156-157)

Prices	Paintings	Countries	Artists
$1,000,000	Baby Jane	Germany	Greta Frank
$2,000,000	Cold Hills	Canada	Inga Howell
$4,000,000	Day of Night	Portugal	Margot Lane
$8,000,000	Forever Blue	France	Hal Garrison
$16,000,000	Awestruck	Spain	Freda Estes
$32,000,000	Eighteen	Norway	Lyle Kramer

The Cat Burglar
(page 158-159)

Years	Cities	Items	Months
1963	London	sapphires	October
1970	Berlin	gold bars	September
1977	Vancouver	emeralds	July
1984	Paris	cash	June
1991	Antwerp	diamonds	April
1998	Seattle	rubies	May

The Final Problem (pages 160-161)

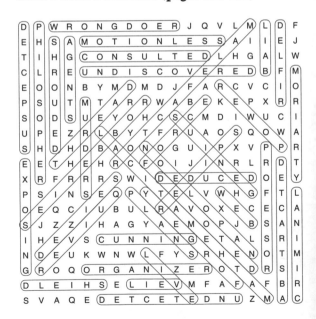

ANSWERS

A "Her Loss Hemlock" Anagram
(page 162)

"It is SIMPLICITY itself," he remarked, chuckling at my surprise, — "so ABSURDLY simple that an explanation is SUPERFLU- OUS; and yet it may serve to define the limits of OBSERVATION and of DEDUCT- TION. OBSERVATION tells me that you have a little reddish mould ADHERING to your instep. Just OPPOSITE the Seymour Street Office they have taken up the PAVEMENT and thrown up some earth which lies in such a way that it is difficult to avoid TREADING in it in entering. The earth is of this pecu- liar REDDISH tint which is found, as far as I know, NOWHERE else in the neighborhood. So much is OBSERVATION. The rest is DE- DUCTION."

"How, then, did you deduce the TELEGRAM _____?"

"Why, of course I knew that you had not WRITTEN a letter, since I sat opposite to you all MORNING. I see also in your open desk there that you have a sheet of stamps and a thick bundle of post-cards. What could you go into the post-office for, then, but to send a wire? ELIMINATE all other FACTORS, and the one which REMAINS must be the truth."

BONUS ANSWER: "The Sign of the Four"

What Went Missing?
(Part I) (page 163)

See part II.

What Went Missing?
(Part II) (page 164)

The bottles and jars on the 4th shelf down on the right had all been taken.

Famous Last Lines
(page 165)

1. E; 2. B; 3. C; 4. D. 5. A

The Con Artist
(pages 166-167)

Months	Names	Towns	Careers
March	Abe Avery	Valero	accountant
April	Fred Flores	Opalville	doctor
May	Matt Mintz	Nanaimo	reporter
June	Sean Starr	Beaverton	bank mgr.
July	Pat Perry	Trippany	dentist
August	Lou Lemon	Hoople	lawyer

ANSWERS

A "Shh Mole Locker" Anagram
(page 168)

"You will remember that I remarked the other day, just before we went into the very SIMPLE problem presented by Miss Mary Sutherland, that for strange effects and EXTRAORDINARY combinations we must go to life itself, which is always far more DARING than any effort of the IMAGINATION."
"A proposition which I took the LIBERTY of DOUBTING."
"You did, DOCTOR, but none the less you must come round to my view, for otherwise I shall keep on PILING fact upon fact on you until your reason breaks down under them and ACKNOWLEDGES me to be right. Now, Mr. Jabez Wilson here has been good enough to call upon me this morning, and to begin a NARRATIVE which promises to be one of the most SINGULAR which I have listened to for some time. You have heard me remark that the STRANGEST and most unique things are very often CONNECTED not with the larger but with the smaller CRIMES, and occasionally, indeed, where there is room for doubt whether any POSITIVE crime has been committed. As far as I have heard it is IMPOSSIBLE for me to say whether the present case is an INSTANCE of crime or not, but the course of events is CERTAINLY among the most SINGULAR that I have ever listened to."

BONUS ANSWER: "The Red-Headed League"

What Went Missing?
(Part I) (page 169)

See part II.

What Went Missing?
(Part II) (page 170)

The compass went missing.